BOOKS CHANGE LIVES

1993 - 1994

Reading Promotion Campaign

COMPILED BY
Michael Thompson

EDITED BY
John Y. Cole, Director
The Center for the Book

LIBRARY OF CONGRESS

WASHINGTON

1996

T A B L E   O F   C O N T E N T S

1993 was the 250th anniversary of the birth of Thomas Jefferson, who insisted that the free and vigorous pursuit of knowledge was essential to a democracy, and to whom the "Books Change Lives" reading promotion campaign was dedicated. A principal founder of the Library of Congress, Jefferson also once told his friend John Adams, "I cannot live without books." This quotation was on the cover of the "Books Change Lives" brochure, which is being admired by Center for the Book consultant Michael Thompson and Jeanne Simon, chair of the National Commission on Libraries and Information Science.

"I Cannot Live Without Books."

THE CENTER FOR THE BOOK

LIBRARY OF CONGRESS

Reading promotion—increasing awareness of the importance of reading for individuals and for society—is one of the most important missions of the Center for the Book in the Library of Congress. At the urging of Librarian of Congress Daniel J. Boorstin, the Center was established in 1977 by Public Law 95-129 to stimulate public interest in books and reading and in the roles that books and reading have played in shaping society. This ambitious purpose was to be accomplished through activities supported by private contributions from individuals, corporations, and foundations.

Today, a national reading promotion network of 30 affiliated state centers and more than 130 national, civic, and educational organizations, all partners of the Center for the Book, help us accomplish our mission. For up-to-date information about state centers, organizational partners, and their reading promotion projects, write the Center for the Book, Library of Congress, Washington, D.C. 20540-4920.

At the 1985 meeting of the Center for the Book's national advisory board, Pat Holt, book review editor of the *San Francisco Chronicle*, suggested that the Library of Congress, through its Center for the Book, sponsor a "Year of the Reader." The year 1987 was so designated—and the Center for the Book's program of national reading promotion campaigns was launched.

"1989—The Year of the Young Reader" brought organizations and individuals concerned with children and young people into the Center's reading promotion network. First Lady Barbara Bush agreed to serve as honorary chair of the "1991-The Year of the Lifetime Reader" campaign, which was described in the Center's publication, *Developing Lifetime Readers: A Report on a National Reading Promotion Campaign* (1993). Mrs. Bush's involvement as honorary chair continued in "Explore New Worlds—READ," our 1992 campaign, which emphasized geography and the literature of travel and exploration. The 1993-1994 theme, "Books Change Lives," is documented in this volume. The latest theme, "Shape Your Future—READ!," continues through 1996.

What is a national reading promotion campaign? How does one participate? Since 1989, an attractive brochure addressing these questions has accompanied each effort, thanks to the generosity of Pizza Hut, Inc., sponsor of the BOOK IT! National Reading Incentive Program in America's Schools. This report—compiled by Center for the Book consultant Michael Thompson, who helps coordinate campaign activities—provides details about how the Books Change Lives project developed and what happened around the country. It also includes contributions from students who participated in "Books Change Lives" essay contests. We hope the essays and report will inspire ideas and participation in reading and literacy campaigns for years to come.

JOHN Y. COLE
Director
The Center for the Book

"Books are the individual's portable, affordable link with the memory, mind, and imagination of the rest of humanity. They link the record of yesterday with the possibilities of tomorrow."

With these words, Librarian of Congress James H. Billington announced that "Books Change Lives" would be the Library of Congress's national reading promotion theme for 1993-1994.

This publication describes how that theme, translated into a reading promotion campaign by the Library's Center for the Book, reached across the United States. It has several purposes:

- to review the events, projects, and activities that took place across the country and made the campaign so popular;
- to make available the ideas that have been proven effective in the promotion of reading;
- to share with a wide audience some of the best and most inspirational statements, ideas, and graphics generated by the campaign;
- and to stimulate thinking on how to make future campaigns even more effective.

The essays in Part I come from three separate essay contests developed by national reading promotion partners of the Library of Congress in cooperation with the Center for the Book.

"Letters About Literature" is a popular annual essay contest for young people organized by Weekly Reader Corporation's Read magazine. Students are asked to write the author of a favorite book, explaining how the book has affected their life. Many of the state centers for the book participate, honoring state winners in ceremonies that often involve prominent state officials. The grand prize is a trip to Washington D.C. that includes a visit to the Library of Congress. More than 10,000 entries were received in the 1993-94 contest. Seven essays from the contest are included in this book, and Conari Press has published a larger selection in *Dear Author: Students Write About the Books That Changed Their Lives* (1995).

Phi Beta Kappa Society's North Texas Association established a "Books Change Lives" essay contest for high school juniors in the Dallas-Fort Worth area, with a $1,000 scholarship for the winner plus a $500 gift to the library in the winner's school. Students were asked to write about how a literary work had affected their life. Seven essays are included from this contest.

The Correctional Education Association developed a "Books Change Lives" essay contest for students enrolled in a GED program. The essay was to "describe how a book, fiction or nonfiction, changed the student's life and should discuss how specific ideas, events or characters in the book suggested that change." Two essays from this contest are included.

Part II of this book focuses on the national "Books Change Lives" campaign, emphasizing the variety of projects and ideas that were conceived or adapted by the Center's reading promotion partners. This was the most popular campaign yet developed by the Center for the Book. One indication is the approximately 15,000 campaign brochures distributed by the Center's office during 1993-1994. Requests came from every state, Guam, the Marshall Islands, the Virgin Islands, and from thirteen countries: Argentina, Australia, Bahamas, Belgium, Canada, England, Ethiopia, Ghana, the Philippines, Scotland, Slovenia, Sri Lanka, and South Africa.

In the appendices, there are lists of books that have changed lives: the books come from the contributors to this volume, from the American Library Association, and from the Center for the Book.

Finally, it should be noted that 1993 was the 250th anniversary of the birth of Thomas Jefferson, who insisted that the free and vigorous pursuit of knowledge was essential to a democracy. He also was a principal founder of the Library of Congress and once told his friend John Adams, "I cannot live without books." Appropriately, "Books Change Lives," the Library's national reading promotion theme for 1993-1994, was dedicated to Jefferson and his belief that education, liberty, and self-government are inseparable.

(Right) From a commemorative poster by Leo and Diane Dillon, commissioned for the "Books Change Lives" campaign by the American Library Association.

BOOKS CHANGE LIVES

Winning Essays and Letters

PART ONE

Center for the Book director John Cole presents Aslum Khan of Rolling Meadows, Ill., grand prize winner of the 1993-1994 "Letters About Literature" contest with a Center for the Book sweatshirt.

I cannot
LIVE
without
BOOKS.

— and Thomas Jefferson agrees.

The Center for the Book in the Library of Congress

President Bill Clinton signs a presidential message commemorating International Literacy Day, Sept. 8, 1994.

on THE OLD MAN AND THE SEA

by Mark Balian, George G. White School, Hillsdale, New Jersey

Mark Balian, a seventh-grade student when he wrote this letter, was a national finalist in Read magazine's 1994-1995 "Letters About Literature" contest.

Dear Mr. Hemingway:
Several weeks ago, my language arts teacher gave us an assignment which required the reading of a novel.

When I mentioned the task to my dad, he went to the basement and brought me a book with a picture of a shack near the shore on the cover.

My first reaction was to ask what the book was about. He replied, "It's a story about an old man, a fish, a Yankee and a few other things."

"What's so special about this book?" I asked. Why should a twelve year old read about an old man? He gave me a "look" that he is famous for, and said, "Even if you don't like the story, maybe you'll learn how to catch a fish, so next time we go to Montauk, we won't come back empty-handed."

With that, my own journey began through what I thought would be a very long 127 pages.

Boy was I wrong! With each page, the pieces all began to fall in place. This wasn't just a story about a fisherman, but a lesson in life!

Over the years my dad had impressed upon me the importance of respect, something called a work ethic, and the need to look at life as a whole and not let any single event cause ups and downs.

This book reinforced these values. It presented an attitude towards life. It reinforced the belief that perseverance and determination are values that cannot be conquered by bad luck.

Joe DiMaggio can be a hero to his fans. However, simple men can become heroes, and being a hero to yourself is as important as being a hero to others.

Most parents encourage you not to give up, and to keep trying. That was certainly the case with me. They gave me tools and opportunity, and most of all, their time. I learned an important lesson in your book. Reach far for your dreams, but know when to quit. Know your limitations, accept them with grace and dignity, then move on with your life.

True, he did catch his marlin. However, the process of life and the laws of nature took over, and the small boat could not keep the sharks from destroying the marlin.

Even in victory, you can lose. One can learn that winning at the expense of something else is not a real victory. We each have a place in life and nature's laws have to be respected.

I see how some things should not carry the importance they do. More importantly, I now see that character, relationships and respect are more meaningful.

Just as the old man learned his limitations and mourned the destruction of his catch, so have I learned to not only set goals, and travel great distances to capture a dream, but to know how to go about achieving them.

The symbolic old shack near the sea on the cover of your book has been able to withstand many storms, so will the valuable lessons of life in your novel.

Yours truly, *Mark Balian*

> BOY WAS I WRONG! WITH
> EACH PAGE, THE PIECES ALL
> BEGAN TO FALL IN PLACE.
> THIS WASN'T JUST A STORY
> ABOUT A FISHERMAN, BUT
> A LESSON IN LIFE!

on IT'S NOT THE END OF THE WORLD

by Annie-Laurie Breen, San Francisco, California

In the seventh grade at St. Gabriel School in San Francisco when she wrote this letter, Annie-Laurie Breen was a finalist in Read magazine's 1994-1995 "Letters About Literature" contest.

Dear Ms. Judy Blume,

Your book, *It's Not the End of the World*, sent me a more powerful message than I have ever received in my life. My parents had been separated for about a year and a half when I first read it, and I still had not accepted that I only lived with one of my parents, instead of both.

Many strong emotions swept over me as I finished the last chapter, the strongest being anger. I was angry with you for making me face the truth—that my parents wouldn't be getting back together, was angry with myself for reading your book. But most of all, I was angry with my parents for becoming like Ellie and Bill.

Weeks later, when I had tamed my anger, disappointment crashed down on me. I was disappointed because of the ending, that at the end Ellie and Bill would not be reunited. In books, there is always a fairy-tale ending. Two people fight, they yell, but at the end, they realize that they still love each other and the live happily ever after. Only it wasn't like that in your book and, unfortunately, it wasn't like that in my life.

It wasn't fair, I decided. It wasn't fair that Karen's and my parents were not together. All of my friends' parents were together, so why was I different? I wasn't going to let on that I cared. That was the final decision that I made. If I kept everything bottled up, maybe the problem would disappear.

I kept things hidden for so long, though, that my mom took us to a family counselor, "Us" meaning herself, my brother, and I. I was convinced that I was fine, that I didn't need to go. After eight sessions, I learned to deal with the brutal truth. Only, after I went, the truth didn't seem so brutal and I didn't feel so alone.

Now, I have a new stepfather and a new brother. I see my father every day when he picks my brother and me up from school. My mother is home after school, and they get along. My father and my stepfather get along, as well. That's not to say that everything is always great. Sometimes one of us is in a bad mood, or someone is overtired. Usually, though, our household runs pretty smoothly.

It was a rough five years, and while things have started to fall in place, some things will never be the same. I will never again wake up at 4:00 a.m. and find my dad in the bathroom, shaving. I will never kiss him before I go to bed each night. He will never have another chance to walk into my bedroom at night and pull down my blinds and turn off my lights. All these things are a part of my childhood, which isn't yet through.

It's Not the End of the World taught me to face my challenges, to share my feelings, and most of all, to have an open mind. From now on, the way that I think will be only temporary. Each time I learn something new, may it be emotionally-wise or school-wise, a little part of me will change. Tomorrow I'll be a different person than I am today, and next week I'll be different than I will be tomorrow.

Throughout my ordeal, my hopes, my dreams, my life have changed dramatically. But one thing will always be the same; no matter how old I get I will still have my memories of helping Dad shave at dawn, and of kissing him each night. I will have memories of climbing into Dad's and Mom's bed.

And do you know something? It's okay that they're just memories. Now I can accept that.

> MANY STRONG EMOTIONS SWEPT
> OVER ME AS I FINISHED THE LAST
> CHAPTER, THE STRONGEST BEING
> ANGER. I WAS ANGRY WITH YOU
> FOR MAKING ME FACE THE TRUTH—
> THAT MY PARENTS WOULDN'T BE
> GETTING BACK TOGETHER.

NIGHT OF HOPE

by Amber Dunn, Nimitz High School, Irving, Texas

This essay won second prize in the 1994-1995 North Texas Association of Phi Beta Kappa's "Books Change Lives" essay contest for high school juniors in the Irving independent school district.

Despair, hope, love, companionship, every one of these feelings came into my heart as I read *Night*, by Elie Wiesel. Two years ago I came to a turning point in my life; I felt lost, and I hated what I had become. My only desire was to be by myself so that I could forget all my problems and pain. My English class was assigned to read *Night* and I remember thinking that it was just one more thing for me to have to do. I never really tried my very best because if you show what you are capable of then it is always expected of you. When I first started to read the book, it dredged up memories I wanted to forget so I chose to skim the rest of it. I managed to pass the tests we had over it, while feeling lost inside. The day before the actual exam I felt I was at an all time low in my life. I prayed for God to help me if he really was there and loved me. I never understood why I picked up that book on that night, but it probably saved my life. I really started to read the words and let myself feel what Elie felt. The more I read the more thankful I became of my surroundings and how truly blessed I really was. I must have sat on that bed for hours just letting the emotions pour out of me. I went to sleep that night with peace, something I had not done in a very long time. I will never comprehend the force that led me to read that book on that fateful night, but I will always be grateful. Now I have worked through my problems and when I start to feel low I reread my copy of *Night* which I purchased shortly after my first real reading. I am thankful that I have my life and my family. Elie truly changed my entire point of view concerning life, and I will forever remember that. Now as I think back to that time of despair I think not of pain and suffering; but instead of hope and joy that I got through it. One day I hope to help someone just as Elie helped me two years ago. The happiness of life and the little things we take for granted day after day, because we do not realize how truly precious they are, came to me through this book. Today I can look back and acknowledge my problems, and when I feel I have reached the end of my rope I merely have to tie a knot and hang on. *Night* is a book that everyone should own and read many times through. This book changed my life and has the ability to change many others too.

I NEVER UNDERSTOOD WHY I PICKED UP THAT BOOK ON THAT NIGHT, BUT IT PROBABLY SAVED MY LIFE.

MY EYES WERE OPENED

by Geoffrey Funk, DeSoto High School, DeSoto, Texas

Geoffrey Funk won second prize in the 1994-1995 essay contest sponsored by the North Texas Association of Phi Beta Kappa for high school juniors in the DeSoto and Duncanville school districts.

I furtively glanced around to see if anyone was watching, then quickly grabbed the book from my brother's desk. It had been a birthday present from a friend of his, but he had yet to begin reading. Titled *Dragonlance Chronicles Volume 1: Dragons of Autumn Twilight*, I was intrigued by the three dissimilar individuals on the cover: one female in a stereotypical Native American outfit, one solemn male in a battered suit of armor, and a second male in a rustic, tanned leather outfit; what caught my eye was the ferocious dragon sneaking up on them from behind.

I continued the journey to my room, but with a more certain purpose now. I lay down on my bed and began reading the prologue...

Being the typical ten-year old child that I was, I had previously seen television as the most imaginative and most exciting source of entertainment in society. The action and suspense of any television show was colossal compared to the ju-venile literature I had read. I felt that if a plot could not be concluded by the two-hundredth page, it was not worth reading. But with *Dragonlance*, it was different. My appetite for adventure was not sated by the two-hundredth page, nor the three-hundredth: I read day and night, and finished the mammoth tome in four days.

After reading the first volume, I had to continue the trilogy, so I proceeded to the second and third volumes, after which I moved on to the next trilogy in the series, and the next, and the next. I branched from The Dragonlance Saga into other fantasy novels. From this point, I introduced myself to science fiction, and then moved on to "classical" literature. *Les Miserables* enthralled me from page one, Machiavelli introduced me to political theory, and Thomas More opened my imagination to the possibility, as well as the plausibility, of Utopian society.

It was not the political, historical, or philosophical importance of *Dragonlance Chronicles Volume 1* that is so important: it was a book that simply opened my mind to the wonders of reading. Margaret Weis and Tracy Hickman, the collaborating authors who created *Dragonlance*, introduced me to the rest of a world which had previously consisted of children's novels (no more than two hundred pages in length), so that Dr. Seuss was replaced by Victor Hugo, so that Matt Christopher was replaced by Gaston Leroux, so that my eyes were opened.

As I look back upon this memory, I realize that the book was not a literary classic. it does not rival the philosophical depth of Victor Hugo's *Les Miserables*, the political statements of Niccolo Machiavelli's *The Prince* or Huxley's *Brave New World*, nor the plot twists of Dickens' *A Tale of Two Cities*, but it was a beginning. The novel caught my imagination, and is still "dragging" me along six years later.

> IT WAS NOT THE POLITICAL, HISTORICAL, OR PHILOSOPHICAL IMPORTANCE OF DRAGONLANCE CHRONICLES VOLUME I THAT IS SO IMPORTANT: IT WAS A BOOK THAT SIMPLY OPENED MY MIND TO THE WONDERS OF READING.

THE DIARY OF ANNE FRANK

by Natasha Gaziano, School, Altamonte Springs, Florida

Natasha Gaziano, an eighth grade student when she wrote this letter, was a national finalists in the 1993-1994 Read magazine "Letters About Literature" contest.

Dear Anne Frank,

I wish you were still alive so I could tell you how deeply your book *The Diary of a Young Girl* affected me. It not only touched my mind but also my soul. Today you would be 64 years old but I visualize you more as a friend my age (13 years old) because we have so many things in common. We both have "dual personalities" that are similar. Also we both like to talk a lot and some people think we are annoying at times. We both have sisters who are beautiful and perfect. Boys, movie stars, and the latest fashions are important to us and math is not our best subject. I think you and I are very funny and like to laugh at humorous things and situations. Most important, we both love life, want to experience everything, and want to be writers.

Anne, your diary taught me and made me think about things that I never thought existed in the world but first of all it made me think about freedom and what it is (or is not) to be free. Being an American we have more freedom than most people in the world. Your diary made me think about how my 13th year differs from yours. I have the freedom to go to a school of my choice, shop at my favorite mall, go to the movies, or go anywhere my parents think is acceptable at any time of the day. Also, I am able to bath, talk, walk, and go to the bathroom any time I want. Most important I have freedom to pursue my dreams. I felt that freedom was what you missed most of all during your 13th year. You taught me how important that is to our existence.

Another lesson that your diary taught me was on discrimination and how terrible it is to treat or mistreat another person because he is different. For the last four months, I have not been able to think about much else other than the way the Jews were treated by the Nazis. I don't think that I was ever discriminated against. But I now try to think before I say something negative about someone, "Will that hurt them?" or "Am I discriminating against them because they are different?"

My parents tell me there is less prejudice and discrimination in the world today than in 1942 but I know it still exists. I, like you, see the world as a place where people are not judged by their religion or the color of their skin. But are judged by the kindness of their heart and their contributions to mankind. I think your quotation, "In spite of everything I still believe that people are really good at heart," shouts your message to the world.

The final lesson that your book taught me is inspiration. In spite of all discrimination, humiliation, and inhumane treatment you showed me the inner strength and courage of a young girl. When things are not going well, I think of your phrase, "Chins up. Stick it out. Better times will come." I think if you can cope with everything, so can I. Some of my classmates said, "How can Anne Frank be an inspiration when in the end she did not fulfill her dreams?" Their statement is somewhat true but your wish, "I want to go on living even after my death," is inspiration to me. You inspired me to realize a young author's words can live forever.

Finally, I would like to tell you that after I read your book, I became so fascinated with World War II and the Holocaust that I have been reading quite a few books on the subject, such as *Anne Frank Remembered*, *The Last Seven Months*, and *Night*. I am also excited to tell you that over my Christmas break from school, as part of my Christmas gift, I will be going to the Holocaust Museum in Washington, DC. There my thoughts will be focused on you and our spirits will touch.

Your friend forever, *Natasha Gaziano*

> I WISH YOU WERE STILL ALIVE SO I COULD TELL YOU HOW DEEPLY YOUR BOOK *THE DIARY OF A YOUNG GIRL* AFFECTED ME. IT NOT ONLY TOUCHED MY MIND BUT ALSO MY SOUL.

THE RUMINATIONS OF A PHILOSOPHER EMPEROR

by Scott Hocutt, Irving High School, Irving, Texas

This essay won first prize in the 1993-1994 "Books Change Lives" essay contest sponsored by the North Texas Association of Phi Beta Kappa for high school juniors in the Irving independent school district.

"...[S]ay and do everything in conformity with the soundest reason." Over 1,800 years ago, Marcus Aurelius, Emperor of Rome, wrote these words in his book, *The Meditations of Marcus Aurelius Antoninus*. Practically all of what he said then is just as relevant now as it was when the Roman Empire stretched from Britannia to Palestine. Marcus Aurelius writes of many things, but he mainly tries to point out the pettiness and impiety of most men in their quest for fame and offers ways for men to correct themselves. However, he values above all else a love of knowledge and philosophy, something I chase so desperately in these times of ignorance and shame.

I first came across Marcus Aurelius while reading a book about evolution on the earth called *Shadows of Forgotten Ancestors*, by Carl Sagan and Ann Druyan. There was a quote in there that stirred me like nothing else had. It read:

> Of human life time is a point, and substance is in a flux, and the perception dull, and the whole body subject to putrefaction, and the soul is a whirl, and fortune hard to divine, and fame a thing devoid of judgement. And, to say all in a word, everything which belongs to the body is a stream, and what belongs to the soul is a dream and vapor, and life is a warfare and a stranger's sojourn, and after-fame is oblivion. What then is that which is able to conduct a man? One thing and only one, the love of knowledge.

Marcus Aurelius's words spoke to me in such a way that I had to read his book, just to see what else he had to say on the pursuit of knowledge. While reading, I found many words of wisdom that most have overlooked in this day and age. The depth of his words made me think quite often about what it is to be a man. Should I lie down trembling at the feet of a god or find out if that god exists? Should I show respect to my fellow man or take advantage of him? Should I show loyalty to my country or wish it a fun trip down the drain? I have thought about these questions and many more as I read this book. Every answer I come up with seems to make me a better person from my point of view. Even the ones that for now remain unanswered are forcing me to think very hard about my future course in life.

From the start, Marcus Aurelius shows great piety toward his ancestors and close acquaintances. In Book I, he lists everyone who has had a profound effect on him and names everything he learned from them and what characteristics he gained as a result of these acquaintances. This attitude of respect for one's acquaintances and reverence toward one's ancestors is something everyone could learn from. From Book II on, it's a whirlwind of everything from advice on life to rhetorical questions that are supposed to make one evaluate just what his morals are.

Marcus Aurelius stresses simplicity in everything we do and say. He wants people to be simple in dress, word, and deed. I have tried to emulate this as best I can in today's overly complex society. Even before reading this book I had seen no point in extravagance, and his words reinforced what I had already believed. He also urges people to examine everything they come across and see how and through what prin-

WHILE I FIND IT IMPOSSIBLE TO DENY MYSELF A SHOT AT IMMORTALITY BY MY ACCOMPLISHMENTS, I SINCERELY HOPE THAT THESE ACCOMPLISHMENTS WILL BE IN THE NAME OF KNOWLEDGE AND NOTHING MORE.

ciple it works. While I am sure this was much easier 1,800 years ago, it is still useful to understand, at least in a basic sense, how all of our modern conveniences work.

Another point that he stresses over and over again is that men should not seek to be remembered after they die, for he feels that in the infinite amount of time in the universe, anyone who remembers will soon die themselves, and all memory of one's achievements will be wiped out. While this may seem to be a depressing philosophy, it really is not, for he believes that men should concentrate on the here and now and focus their resources on the betterment of society through one's own small, but beneficial, contributions to society. While this may seem almost repulsive at first, it is only because it goes against our strongest instinct: survival. Everyone wants immortality, whether they try to find a god or heaven in which to believe, whether they prefer to be remembered for their accomplishments by future generations, or both. While I find it impossible to deny myself a shot at immortality by my accomplishments, I sincerely hope that these accomplishments will be in the name of knowledge and nothing more.

The most moral message that I received from this book was always to be good to my fellow man. While not exactly espousing turning the other cheek, he continually repeats the need to be a good, moral person towards society in general. He continually says how no harm is done if no harm is taken. This is so true, for being vengeful for petty reasons only brings about ruin and an early death from stress.

What, then, must I have learned by reading these wonderfully formulated, well-thought-out, very articulated arguments? I believe that I have learned to show respect to my fellow citizen, to be simple in my living but not in my thinking, to avoid overindulgence, to seek not fame but knowledge, and to always attempt anything that will prove fruitful in life, for I have only a short amount of time to accomplish my goal of becoming an astronomer and unraveling the many secrets of the universe, many of which Marcus Aurelius had no idea of in his time. However, he touched on many of the deepest questions of the universe, including what makes a man, what makes man's consciousness, and whether the universe is actually infinite. In the end, however, it all comes down to whether I think I lived a fruitful life, and I hope I can prove to be worthy of the following:

"Consider if thou hast hitherto behaved to all in such a way that this may be said of thee: *Never has wronged a man in deed or word.*"

ONE BOOK, ONE LIFE

by Aslum Khan, Rolling Meadows High School, Rolling Meadows, Illinois

A senior at the time he wrote this letter, Aslum Khan won the Grand Prize in Read magazine's 1993-1994 "Letters About Literature" contest.

Dear Mr. Haley,
"Who was Malcolm X?"

The entire eighth-grade English class sat silent at Mrs. Pfeiffer's question. I didn't have a clue. Nobody seemed to. We listened to the heater hum, and if it had been a scene from a cartoon, we would have heard crickets.

Then, Roshawn Watson, a dapper black friend of mine, raised his hand and explained. "You know how Martin Luther King wanted blacks to be nonviolent? Malcolm kind of told them to fight back if necessary."

That was it. That was my introduction to Malcolm X. The movie and the T-shirts were still years away, there was no hype surrounding him, and yet, something intrigued me about this man. At first, I was horrified at Roshawn's response, amazed that there was actually a black man who told blacks to fight back against whites. Who would say such a thing?

Two years passed. My mother had died, and my father and I were on poor terms. I didn't feel like going on. I thought I didn't have much chance for future success. I was Indian and a Muslim, and everyone knows how Americans feel about those who are different. You are an outsider. A stranger. Nobody wants you. You can make as many white friends as you want, but when it comes right down to it, they're American; you're not.

All those feelings changed after I read your book.

The wound of my mother's death was still sore. I needed somebody—something—to tell me my life wasn't over. That my mother, with all of her ideals and her outlandish behavior, was not crazy. That she was a normal human being. I didn't think Malcolm had ANYTHING to do with her. I was wrong.

Malcolm X was so like my mother and like what I strive to be, it astonished me. Here was a man who was so different from everybody, so defiant and so honest, that whether or not people liked him became irrelevant. They RESPECTED him. He was a Muslim in a time when nobody had ever heard of Islam. He was an ex-con who fooled scholars into thinking he had a college education just by reading books. And most of all, he was honest and had the strength to change when he knew he was wrong.

Suddenly everything my mother had told me about honesty, doing well in school and not following the crowd had new meaning to me. Malcolm derived his strength purely by the knowledge that he was doing the right thing. He had unquestioning confidence in himself, and all the things that made me an outcast were HIS strengths. He was a Muslim. He changed the word from meaning "that weird foreign religion" to "watch out for these guys. They have ATTITUDE." Malcolm X would tell the whole world to kiss his…Well, he wouldn't say it that way. He believed that foul language was for those who could not express themselves. After getting out of prison, he played everything by the rules and never broke a law again, but he could provoke more anger from society than a mass murderer.

But the thing that touched me the most about Malcolm is how, behind this tough demeanor, he really was a normal, nice person. He knew when he was wrong; he always searched for the truth. He lived a clean life under Allah's teachings, even if those teachings cost him his own life. That's a martyr. That's a hero.

You can't measure the amount of strength I got out of your book, Mr. Haley. It's something I feel even as I walk down the street. I realize now that I am a talented, good person, and nobody can tell me otherwise. I know that there's nothing to fear from society. You can't live your life trying to do what others tell you to do. Now I know, as my mother tried to teach me time and again before she died, that you can't go wrong with truth.

Thank you for the greatest book I have ever read, *The Autobiography of Malcolm X*.

> YOU CAN'T MEASURE THE AMOUNT OF STRENGTH I GOT OUT OF YOUR BOOK, MR. HALEY. IT'S SOMETHING I FEEL EVEN AS I WALK DOWN THE STREET.

LOVE, UNITY, AND PATIENCE = VICTORY IN LIFE

by Veronica Lee, Duncanville High School, DeSoto, Texas

This is the winning essay in the 1994-1995 "Books Change Lives" essay contest sponsored by the North Texas Association of Phi Beta Kappa for high school juniors in the DeSoto and Duncanville independent school districts.

Throughout the course of life one will encounter some type of book at some particular point. Whether this book is a collection of poems, short stories, a novel, or some other form of literary work it will have an effect on the individual that encounters it. Perhaps the person may be bored or excited, feel sad or happy, confused or understanding, frightened or confident, loving or hating, etc. Whatever the case, the person will develop some type of relationship with the book, or opinion towards the contents of the book. Mildred D. Taylor's *Roll of Thunder, Hear My Cry* has changed my life by allowing me to be able to sympathize and empathize with my ancestors, by furthering my awareness of history, and by encouraging me to aim higher to pursue change for the better in my life.

First of all the verisimilitude of the work allows me to sympathize and empathize with my ancestors and the circumstances that they encountered in their generations and lifetimes. Verisimilitude is created by the realness of characters and their lifestyles. The Logan family is a black family struggling to overcome rural Southern racism during the Depression. All they strive to do is to be free. They do not bother anyone. They are loving, sharing, law-abiding citizens that just want to have rights and privileges like other humans have and enjoy. However, the mere color of their skin alienates them from the level of normal human beings and places them on so low a level that some animals are not treated as horribly as they are. The reason I can sympathize and empathize with my ancestors is a direct result of this fact, because I, being a young black girl myself, know what it feels like for someone else to put me down and try to make me feel inferior.

Furthermore, my awareness of my history was deepened by the fact that I was learning about the way two cultures lived and the way these cultures accepted each other. Although blacks were made to feel inferior, they were able to maintain strong family ties and love in their hearts for the oppressor. In this light I was able to better understand how and why Dr. Martin Luther King, Rosa Parks, and all the other civil rights activists (both black and white) were able to fight nonviolently for equality. They understood that the oppressors did have a heart but they really believed that they were superior. They understood that God was on their side and that eventually they, as a race, would overcome. In the same light, the Logan family knows that better days are ahead if they stay together and keep love in their heart. Before, I could not fully comprehend how people survived in history and now my mind and knowledge have been opened to love, unity, and patience being the key to survival.

Also, I was encouraged to do more in my life to let myself and others know that we are overcomers. If a being is a human, alive and breathing, then no matter what condition his or her physical qualities may be, he or she is no greater or any less than any other human. We all need to love, even though people come against us and try to keep us down. It is then that we should love the most and do our best to help each other find their love and peace, so that, in the future, they will be able to apply these characteristics to their lives. I am now en-

> FURTHERMORE, MY AWARENESS OF MY HISTORY WAS DEEPENED BY THE FACT THAT I WAS LEARNING ABOUT THE WAY TWO CULTURES LIVED AND THE WAY THESE CULTURES ACCEPTED EACH OTHER.

couraged to spread the message and share my success with others so that life for someone else may be a little more pleasant.

Lastly, although *Roll of Thunder, Hear My Cry* is a children's book, it has greatly influenced my life. Besides, I was a child when I read it. I am now a teenager and I have experienced reading novels that require much deeper thought, however, I do not feel that any of these have had a greater impact in my life than that of this particular book. It was a deeply moving, very insightful book, even being a children's book, which I will cherish as a part of my life forever.

on A TREE GROWS IN BROOKLYN

by Hae Jung Moon, Nimitz High School, Irving, Texas

Hae Jung Moon's essay won third prize in the North Texas Alliance of Phi Beta Kappa's 1993-1994 contest for high school juniors in the Irving independent school district.

As a little girl growing up, curious of the changing days in life, I learned more from reading books, that there is more to life than what I can see. Curling up and escaping into fictitious fantasies, a book made me use my imagination to create in my mind what the characters or settings look like. However, the novel, *A Tree Grows in Brooklyn*, taught me to face the realities of life.

"There's a tree that grows in Brooklyn. It grows lushly . . . survives without sun, water, and seemingly without earth" (Smith). In a world full of growing trends for an introspective existence, one must succeed with wealth to survive. However, that tree represents the thousands of people who possess nothing, yet have everything in life in order to grow and survive. The tree also represents the little girl in the novel, Francie, who lives in the slums of New York, but manages to live on the love and support of her family. Although I first read this book as only an eighth grader, with still a lot of growing-up to do, it made me realize that there were other people struggling to survive. I felt the pain and happiness the girl went through as she witnessed her alcoholic father die, saw her mother give birth, and felt the ache of a broken heart.

The author did justice in creating a character that is so real that any girl can admire and love her. I admire the strength and courage of the heroine for teaching me that nothing can stand in the way of my goals and dreams, and to ignore all the criticism. Francie had no money and no materialistic things. She was shunned from society. Yet, her courage allowed her to overcome being molested by a stranger; her valor kept her alive after the death of her father; her spirit brought light into her family at times of despair; and her determination got her into college.

I also learned from her mistakes that although I should not easily trust another soul, there are warm friends out there who are willing to lend all a hand. The book taught me to make the best of a situation. Sure, Francie had no wealth, but she had a fulfilling childhood full of happy memories. These kids in the slums created their own games, their own rituals. Most importantly, Francie indulged in books to educate herself and to escape the pain.

The novel made me thankful for what I have and led me to wonder if I could survive with only the basic essentials. Francie survived without money, an unofficial requirement in society. The tree in Brooklyn survived without the sun or water, a necessity for life. So, yes, I can survive on my own no matter how much I have or do not have.

> THE TREE IN BROOKLYN SURVIVED WITHOUT THE SUN OR WATER, A NECESSITY FOR LIFE. SO, YES, I CAN SURVIVE ON MY OWN NO MATTER HOW MUCH I HAVE OR DO NOT HAVE.

Reading one book opened my eyes to the world and taught me so much of the beauty of life. A book can bring so much to a girl wanting to escape the cruelty of life. I have truly been touched by *A Tree Grows in Brooklyn*, because I am a girl still maturing and learning about survival. I will always remember the tree that struggled to reach the sky. I am that tree, struggling for life, but comforted by knowing that I can control my destiny by never letting anything pull me down.

on INSIDE TRACK

by Katherine Niblett, Laguna Middle School, San Luis Obispo, California

This letter, which Katherine Niblett an eighth grade student entered in Read magazine's 1994-95 "Letters About Literature" contest, earned her the contest's Grand Prize.

Dear Mr. Lewis,

Well, I'm in school now and back on track. Last year I dropped out. Thanks to your book, *Inside Track*, I was given the inspiration to, as you put it, "look forward." Initially, I selected your book because we have common interests in sports and running. After reading the first two chapters, I realized we shared much more.

I am a shy runt, too, just like you said you were. You might have been the smallest in your family, but last year I was the smallest in my whole school. At 4'6" most kids considered me the school nerd. They pushed me around the halls, stole my glasses, and in general made life miserable. As you know, prejudice comes in all forms.

A lot happened and I could not handle it. I ached with that hollow emptiness you expressed with the loss of your father. In April, my grandfather died. I left school last year drifting without direction.

Sports have always been my life. It was the only thread I had to hang onto. I don't have a team or a coach. I only have my younger brother Michael. We play in the same way you did, setting up track meets in our yard. I had to laugh about how you handed out your Mom's medals at your meets. I bet she laughs now too even though she didn't then. You spoke with such love and affection about your parents. I feel the same about my family. Unlike you, my parents are not athletes, but they help us all they can.

> THE OFFICIAL DASHED MY DREAMS LIKE BEN JOHNSON HAD SHATTERED YOURS. BY JUNE, I REACHED AN ALL-TIME LOW. THEN I DISCOVERED YOUR BOOK.

A big race was coming up. It wasn't your Olympics, but for me it was just as important. The Arizona Iron Kids Triathlon Race was the place I wanted to carry home a victory in memory of my grandfather. I think you could understand since you expressed a desperate need to bring the gold home in your dad's honor after his death. Usually we don't travel much to races. It is too expensive. Mom and Dad knew what this one meant to me so it was a go. Grandmother came for support. I was ready, but nervous. It was good to hear even the pros like you get on edge before a race.

I got off to a great start and was out of the swimming pool well in front of my competition. I held the lead on the first bike loop. I knew I could outrun my field. All I needed was a respectable bike time. As I came into the bike marking zone, the official accidentally hooked me with his arm as he marked the inside of my elbow instead of the outside of my arm. All 80 pounds of me went flying over the front of my handle bars along with my dreams of a win for grandfather.

My right side slammed into the pavement. Blood streamed from my shoulder to my ankle. Ambulance drivers tried to assist me, but I shoved them away and got back on my bike. The sportsmanship award I received wasn't the gold I had worked so hard for. Like you, I just wanted to run the race I had trained for. The official dashed my dreams like Ben Johnson had shattered yours. By June, I reached an all-time low. Then I discovered your book.

It was like a light bulb flashed on. You explained so many things that were brewing inside me about life and sports. I wasn't alone any more. You were there with me. Your book taught me size and circumstances don't matter as much as goals and persistence.

You said you had a turning point in your sophomore year when you messed up for your teammates. If Carl Lewis could mess up and turn it around, I began to think I could, too. As I turned the pages, you became a friend to me because you understood how I felt.

People think you just go out and run. The clock is the only enemy. We know there is so much more to it. Drugs, politics, press, coaches, peers, and more all effect the outcome of a race, and life.

Inside Track really turned things around for me. I started working even harder on my training and academics by setting realistic goals and striding ahead. Over the summer, my brother and I helped to earn enough to go to the Youth Triathlon National Championships in Nashville. It was our first national race. I thought a lot about what advice you would give me. Your book echoed, "Just run your race. Focus."

Mr. Lewis, I did just that. I wish I could tell you I won the triathlon, but I can't. I am proud to say, though, I beat the winner's swim by 18 seconds and outran her by 7 seconds. My run was the fastest ranked run of the senior girls in the United States at the national championships.

You helped me to run in the right direction. The warm, honest sharing of your experiences has given me the courage to go beyond pain and frustration. Frankness regarding what you experienced encouraged me to risk whatever the future holds. *Inside Track* is an inspiration and guiding light to me.

BOOKS DO CHANGE LIVES

by Shelly Novotny, Nimitz High School, Irving, Texas

This was the winning essay in the North Texas Association of Phi Beta Kappa's 1994-1995 "Books Change Lives" essay contest for high school juniors in the Irving independent school district.

Books *do* have a tremendous effect on people's lives. The simple story I read that altered my way of thinking and behaving was about an act of loyalty and love so profound that the matters of the world became inconsequential. *Where the Red Fern Grows*, by Wilson Rawls, tells of a boy, Billy, whose one dream in life is to have hunting dogs of his own to train and love. Through perseverance and patience, his wish comes true. His dogs, Old Dan and Little Ann, soon create a partnership that cannot be matched. The love that grows among these three becomes threaded so intimately in their hearts that, when the life of the young boy is threatened, Old Dan sacrifices his own life to save him. Little Ann lives only a few days after that because she is so filled with loneliness. Billy is overwhelmed with grief, and soon after he buries the dogs side by side, a red fern sprouts between them. Billy remembers that as a boy his mother used to tell him of an Indian brother and sister who became lost in a blizzard and froze to death. When they were found, a red fern had grown between them. Indian legend says that only love and loyalty can nurture it.

As a child I never knew the depth of sorrow or love. Unhappiness to me simply was not being able to sleep in on Saturday morning. The desolation in my life began the day my father decided to walk out of our lives. To rebel, I became a hellion in every way. I do not believe I let his leaving affect me until one night in my family's rental house, I watched my

THE SIMPLE STORY I READ THAT ALTERED MY WAY OF THINKING AND BEHAVING WAS ABOUT AN ACT OF LOYALTY AND LOVE SO PROFOUND THAT THE MATTERS OF THE WORLD BECAME INCONSEQUENTIAL.

mother sleep. I realized then that honest love is so scarce in this world that, when it is found, it needs to be grasped tightly. She looked so vulnerable that I decided right there, at only 12, that I needed to grow up and take care of her. An anguish that I had never felt before flooded into me, and, just like Billy, I had to face the facts that I understood what no child should ever have to understand. I realized that sorrow and acceptance are apart of life, but we must persevere or be lost in the oncoming waves. I also realized the power of prayer. Billy had prayed for someone to love, and his mother had prayed for the happiness of her family; in turn, I prayed for the strength to change and unite with my family to fight through this. We are better now—my mother has remarried; my brother is going to college, and I have grown up and now find myself in the top ten percent of my class. Still, I will never forget the moment I made parallel between this book and my life. Today, I understand how meaningful reading can be. Books do change lives, and I have Wilson Rawls to thank for helping me truly understand "where the red fern grows."

on SAY GOODNIGHT, GRACIE

by Natalie Prado, East Lansing High School, East Lansing, Michigan

Natalie Prado became a national finalist in Read magazine's 1994-1995 "Letters About Literature" contest.

Dear Ms. Julie Reece Deaver,
I would like to thank you for your book, *Say Goodnight, Gracie*. I first read it a couple of years ago and (young as I was) I found it depressing and missing the air of romance that I at that time craved. It seems ironic to look back on my attitude then, because now I can realize that it is, in fact, a love story. Not because it was romantic or exotic at all, but because it tells about love and loss in a way I didn't understand then.

Love was a word that I thought I knew all about and that I looked upon in reverence. At the time, I was overlooking the only sort of love I knew, that I did not know the extent of. It was May of that year that I had a theater performance. Distinctly I remember falling asleep that night, exhausted and ecstatic.

The next morning my parents woke me up and told me my brother was dead.

Grief and pain have blocked out most of May and June, I can no longer remember them. Now, so much later, I have to strain to remember exactly how my brother was before the accident. Only small things remain clear. His smile. His eyes.

Suddenly other things invaded my life, and I began to feel the need to pull my family back together. My parents would cry openly. I remember my mother on her knees before my grandmother, rocking and screaming, "Mommy! Mommy! My baby's dead! My baby's dead!"

My poor, frightened younger brother and sisters would cry in confusion, and in frustration. They could barely understand what was happening and I was too stunned and angry to help them.

Until my brother died, there were many things I did not understand. The most important is that I loved my brother. The most painful is that I never got a chance to tell him so. I would give anything in the world to tell him how much I loved him and needed him and how much I miss him.

Two weeks ago I found your book in the library of my grief-counselling center. I checked it out and spent the entire night reading it and crying. I more than understood the feelings Morgan had after Jimmy's death. I recognized them as my own. When my brother died I became very depressed, even (at times) suicidal. Your book had something that I missed the first time I read it: a message of hope. By the end Morgan knew that however terrible Jimmy's death was he would live through it. You were right; there are people in our lives we don't think we will ever live without. I have learned our very strength is that we can.

YOUR BOOK HAD SOMETHING THAT I MISSED THE FIRST TIME I READ IT: A MESSAGE OF HOPE. BY THE END MORGAN KNEW THAT HOW-EVER TERRIBLE JIMMY'S DEATH WAS HE WOULD LIVE THROUGH IT.

on THE JUNGLE

by Seth Rothey, Findlay High School, Findlay, Ohio

Seth Rothey was a sophomore when he entered this letter and became a national finalist in Read magazine's 1994-1995 "Letters About Literature" contest.

I am a 5'10" 175-pound robust guy who plays football and ice hockey. Most people wonder how I got so big in the first place, for I am a vegetarian. I am not quite sure how this all happened, but I have never enjoyed meat. My mom told me even as a baby I would spit the meat out when she tried to feed me. It has been quite a long time since I have had red meat, like steak, probably around eight or nine years. I have had to put up with numerous tauntings either at lunch, when I order my "veggie" cheeseburgers, or at football dinners, when I pass up the spaghetti with meat sauce. My meat consumption consists of a Chicken McNugget here and there or a chicken wing or taco as a dare. I stick to my practice, though. People ask me all the time, "How can you live without meat?" My only reply is that I have never lived with meat, so it's easy. "Why don't you like it?" In response to this other popular question I reply, "I don't know, I just don't." Most people look at vegetarians as torturing themselves like people who give up candy for Lent. I just have never relished meat. For years I have stared at my friends as they bite into a hamburger or a taco at a fast food joint. I cringe at the thought of what additives are included in that "meat". They just counter my scowling with a snide remark or two such as, "Wanna come over tonight for a steak dinner?" But most people have learned and grown to respect my eating habits over time.

After reading your book *The Jungle*, I have a renewed cause for avoiding meat. I read in wonder, most times horror, of the practices of the meat packing companies. How, when a man fell into the meat traps, he was just ground up and sent away with all the other meat. The addition of the diseased and rotten meat to the "good" meat allowed by the inspectors was a horrifying practice. It is no wonder many people became sick, and the death of little Kristofaras occurred apparently after eating a sausage link. I am now glad I have not eaten a hamburger, taco, or other meat for quite a while. This book told of the secrecy about the disease-infected meat around 1906. Who knows if this same conspiracy might be in progress at this very time?

The book also deals with the troubles and struggles of the poor, something very new to me. Throughout my life I have never had to worry where I will stay or what I will live on to the next day. I have never had to give every cent to my name in the effort to obtain the bare essentials of life. The family in *The Jungle* came to America with prosperity and wealth dancing in their heads. Yet, upon arrival, these hopes and dreams were smashed. I have never been able to relate to these tragic lifestyles until now. Being an average middle-class citizen, reading this story of this good-natured family thrown into the deep abyss of poverty was depressing. What makes it even more savage and horrible is that it is no less of a factor now as it was then. I can still remember my glancing away from beggars as they pleaded for "just a dime for a cup of warm coffee." Now I will happily drop a quarter into the dirty styrofoam cup of the coatless unfortunate person. Thank you for a life-enforcing, life-changing book.

Sincerely, *Seth Rothey*

> NOW I WILL HAPPILY DROP A QUARTER INTO THE DIRTY STYROFOAM CUP OF THE COATLESS UNFORTUNATE PERSON. THANK YOU FOR A LIFE-ENFORCING, LIFE-CHANGING BOOK.

The Effect of
THE AUTOBIOGRAPHY OF MALCOLM X

by Rickey Smith, Sumter Correctional Institution, Florida

This was the winning essay in the 1993-1994 essay contest sponsored by the Correctional Education Association for inmates enrolled in GED classes. It has also appeared in the Association newsletter, CEA News and Notes as a cover article and in Reading Today, the biweekly newspaper of the International Reading Association.

Before I expand on why I feel this book, *The Autobiography of Malcolm X*, has had such a profound effect upon me and my life, I would like to give the reader of this essay an idea of the situation at the time I came into contact with this book. Maybe you will be better able to understand why I was able to relate to the character of this book, Malcolm Little, so well.

At the time I came into contact with this book, I was in jail for robbery, the result of a drug addiction. I had lost touch with reality and all of my hopes and dreams. I had no love for self and no understanding for self. Normally in jail, the first book one comes in contact with is the Holy Bible. The Bible is always waiting in a cold and lonely cell to save a lost soul.

But the book that was waiting for this lost soul was *The Autobiography of Malcolm X*. I don't mind telling you I was not a big reader. For some reason, I could not and would not put that book down. I found myself at night, after lights were out, standing by the cell door, trying to catch hold of any light I could to read by. As I write this essay, I find myself deeply searching for the words to accurately describe the effect on me of the character of the book, Malcolm Little (later known by the street name Detroit Red), street hustler, dope dealer, and addict.

I could relate to the characters of the book. I was that street hustler; I was that dope dealer; I was also that dope fiend. The book was no longer a book; it transformed itself into a mirror; it became my life story. The more I read, and the deeper I got into the book, the better the understanding I got of my self, my situation, and my condition.

And as I read, I realized a change coming over the character of Malcolm Little. He commented on how deeply the religion of Islam "had reached down into the mud to lift him up, to save him from being what he inevitably would have been." For some reason beyond my understanding at the time, that statement embedded itself in my mind and it awakened something within me. That statement made me realize that I was a threat…to myself. "Saved me" is a very deep statement. When one is living the so-called street life, the life of a hustler or dope dealer, you never really think of yourself as needing to be saved from anything. That fast life has a unique way of making one feel as if he is on top of the world.

What I got from the book, *The Autobiography of Malcolm X*, no amount of money could buy. That book compelled me to find out more about the religion of Islam. From my study of the Quran, I found my human feelings restored. The religion of Islam is about brotherhood, respect for self, and respect for all other human beings. The religion of Islam teaches us to judge man not by color, but by his character and actions.

What I got from *The Autobiography of Malcolm X* is a new start on life. I have changed my views about society; I now respect self and others. In the autobiography, Malcolm realized the need to obtain an education. He realized that he suffered not because of what he knew, but because of what he didn't know. He realized education was the best possible way to change his condition and to reform and refine his mind. Malcolm saw education as a tool that could be used to elevate as well as cultivate his mind; he saw education as a way to lift himself out of the mud.

After reading that book, *The Autobiography of Malcolm X*, I realized I was reading about a man who was once in the same situation as myself, who

> THE BOOK WAS NO LONGER
>
> A BOOK; IT TRANSFORMED
>
> ITSELF INTO A MIRROR; IT
>
> BECAME MY LIFE STORY.

was once on the same level as myself. That book made me realize the potentials I have within me, the potentials to bring about change, the potentials to live a better life, a more productive life. That book incited something within me; it awakened something within me that had been sleeping for a very long time. At that time, I really could not understand the feelings that came over me after reading that book. But they were feelings of hope, a respect for self, and an understanding for self.

A feeling inside of me that told me everything was going to be all right, a feeling that told me I could and would be someone. That book made me realize that I could turn my life around. And in closing, I would like to say, I am now seeking to obtain my G.E.D., and I now read voraciously from philosophy to psychology. I have a deep love for reading, and a newfound respect for education.

ESCAPE FROM THE DARK AGES

by David Taylor, MacArthur High School, Irving, Texas

This essay won the second prize in the 1993-1994 essay contest sponsored by the North Texas Alliance of Phi Beta Kappa for high school juniors in the Irving independent school district.

The Dark Ages, the period of time during which Western Europe was marred by hopeless ignorance, putrid squalidness, and extreme barbarism, remains to this day a black-eye on the world timeline. The age included the removal of public education, a decrease in artistic and technical skills, and the proliferation of stories and rumors accepted as facts. The black-eye lasted over 500 years. But what caused the Dark Ages? How could knowledge from ancient civilizations disappear? What is to blame? The answers lie in the fact that almost all erudite literature was destroyed or lost during this era. The infamous effects of the absence of books prove the outstanding importance of literature in our world.

Living in a time and place where books are highly accessible has allowed my desire for knowledge to be fulfilled. One book that has affected my life is J.R.R. Tolkien's novel *The Lord of the Rings*. The work of fiction captured my imagination and vaulted me into the land of Middle Earth while, at the same time, challenging my way of thinking.

First, Tolkien showed me the boundlessness of the human imagination. I lived the adventure with all the story's characters. I saw Bilbo disappear at this spectacular birthday party. I travelled on horseback with Frodo during his frightful escape into Rivendell from the Riders. I was with Gandalf just before he plunged to his death in the mines of Moria. I trembled with Sam as he watched Gollum carry the One Ring to its destruction on Mount Doom. I was there!

Tolkien stirred my perception of the human imagination. The fantasy stretched my understanding by presenting unique predicaments, places, and people. My mind was challenged to create pictures of the beautiful and sometimes absurd pictures the words detailed. After reading the novel, I am more adept at visualizing foreign situations and abstract concepts.

Now it is easier for me to relate to friends explaining their personal problems or to comprehend difficult mathematical diagrams. Newspaper articles no longer pose as obstacles to my insight concerning contemporary issues. By exercising my mind's imagination, my work has broadened my scope of understanding. The implementation of a broad and creative imagination can open the door to new inventions, and inventiveness is what imagination is all about. Tolkien's far-fetched fantasy pushed the limits of my comprehension and creativity.

The Lord of the Rings also taught me the importance of skilled and knowledgeable leadership. Gandalf, the aged and experienced wizard, led the small band on its way to the land of Mordor. From escaping sure death by defeating the Balrog at the Battle of the Peak to predicting the one and only way to destroy the One Ring, Gandalf displayed the skill and wisdom all leaders need to develop. The scholarly and clever magician saw himself and his companions through trial after trial.

> I TREMBLED WITH SAM AS HE WATCHED GOLLUM CARRY THE ONE RING TO ITS DE-STRUCTION ON MOUNT DOOM. I WAS THERE!

A leader must develop certain characteristics in order to be effective. First, the leader must learn and keep learning. Studying books, examining past events, and learning through experience are several paths to take. Most importantly, a great leader must never stop acquiring knowledge because, with knowledge, one's wisdom can be used to its potential. Next, a great leader will set an example through his own actions. When his followers see his exemplary behavior, positive responses to similar situations will result. The book encouraged me to keep learning all I can and to demonstrate my leadership qualities.

Lastly, the novel illustrates the invaluable rewards of completing one's quest. The Fellowship of the Ring reached its goal of destroying the One Ring and the Dark Lord. As a result, notoriety, wealth, and satisfaction came their way. Frodo and his companions fulfilled the most important event of their lives and enjoyed the accompanying results.

Reaching one's goal causes several short-term effects. Success can breed fame, but fame cannot totally satisfy. Achievement can generate money, but money cannot buy happiness. What long-term effect accomplishment can and should create is self-fulfillment. Self-fulfillment brings peace, which is the removal of troublesome emotions, and happiness, which is contentment. My quest is to achieve the most complete education and perform my personal best at everything I attempt. Graduating from college and doing so with honors will be my preliminary goals. Looking forward to my own success, the only rewards I truly desire are self-fulfillment, peace, and happiness.

Taking advantage of the absence of any Dark Age, I am able to acquire and read thought-provoking literature at my own will. *The Lord of the Rings* affected my thinking and influenced my life. Tolkien's masterpiece pointed me towards the world of imagination, suggested qualities of leadership, and revealed the positive aspects of achieving an objective. I am thankful for my opportunity to gain knowledge through books, and I am hopeful that others will also take advantage of the often overlooked convenience of libraries.

HOW MAYA ANGELOU'S CHILDHOOD AND HARDSHIPS AFFECTED MY LIFE

by Jimmie Willoughby, Medium Security Facility, Lorton, Virginia

This is the winning essay in the 1994-1995 essay contest co-sponsored by the Correctional Education Association and the Bureau of Federal Prisons for inmates enrolled in GED courses.

I am writing about how Maya Angelou in her book, *I Know Why the Caged Bird Sings*, inspired me. In her book, there were three things that affected my life; these were things such as growing up in the church, respecting one another, experiencing racism and desiring a good education. These things have made me a better person. I am not about racism anymore. I am inspired by Maya to further my education and respect people. I believe in God and I pray.

During her childhood, Maya was brought up in the church. Going to church played a big part of my childhood too. Almost every Sunday, I would be in the church. Sometimes I went to Sunday school. That's when I realized there was a God and also believed in God. There was no going to sleep or playing in church. Now, today, the church has taught me right from wrong.

There was a time when Maya Angelou had seen the hatred that Klansmen brought to Black people. Hatred and racism have affected me in a period of my life. I could not understand why races of people could not get along and respect each other. Peer pressure at one point in my life taught me to dislike white people. I believe that I have never hated anyone. People all around me were acting the same way, hating or disliking other races. Other races acted like they thought they were better than we were.

This act of racism slowed down my determination to strive for more education or better jobs. Also I had low self-esteem. I was taught that people were better than I was. Today, I realized that people may have more money or material things than I have, but they are not better. I can have the same things. We are all humans. Today, everybody should love one another. Racism affected my life in such a way that I turned to crime and drugs and was later sent to prison. Today, I have a better understanding of life;

crime and drugs will keep people of all races in prisons or cemeteries.

Maya Angelou was taught respect in her childhood. When I was growing up as a child and now today as a young man, I try to respect all people I come in contact with. People will like me more or give me the same respect back. My life has changed since I respect people more. There were times I would get into fights or get punished for disrespecting someone. I understand that I am not perfect, but I usually try to respect people. I have learned that in respecting others good things have happened to me. I also feel better about myself.

After the jobs Maya had in her upbringing, she still got an education. She seemed determined to get an education no matter what. Education affects my life today; that is to say, I will continue my education. In my earlier years I quit high school and went to the Job Corps and the Army Reserve. I did not further my education. I am inspired today to continue my education whether it be in this school or at home. Education to me is never too late to learn something. I am striving to be the best I can be.

By overcoming some of the hardships of my life, I have a better outlook on life that I once did. I have learned more and I know what I am capable of doing. I am patient and determined to enjoy my life and to "do the right things."

In conclusion, through hardships both Maya and I have made it. My life is getting somewhat better. I have overcome the racism. I have love for my brother man now. I respect people more. I do favors for someone who is not asking for something in return. I am getting closer to the creator which I call God. I pray to him and have faith in him. This was something that I had forgotten about at one time in my life.

> I AM NOT ABOUT RACISM
> ANYMORE. I AM INSPIRED
> BY MAYA TO FURTHER MY
> EDUCATION AND RESPECT
> PEOPLE. I BELIEVE IN GOD
> AND I PRAY.

In conjunction with its national reading promotion campaign and belief that books truly change lives, the Center for the Book in the Library of Congress and the Library's Publishing Office produced a traveling display called "Books That Shaped America." Available through Social Issues Resources Series (SIRS) of Boca Raton, Florida, the display—part of a Library of Congress Corner series—traces the powerful influence books have had in American life from the birth of the nation during the Enlightenment to the mass dissemination of print matter we have at our fingertips today.

BOOKS ARE FOR KIDS

Horatio Alger, Jr. wrote over 100 boys' tales, including *Tattered Tom* (1871). These instructional fictions, loosely based on Alger's own rise from editor to corporate president, extolled the "American Dream" and exalted personal virtues. Rare Book and Special Collections Division.

Prior to the modern efforts of writers like James Welch and N. Scott Momaday, American Indian literature was primarily transmitted by spoken word. Among the many Indian storytellers who have passed along a deeper knowledge of Indian folklore was Waihusiwa, a Zuni whose tales were transcribed in *Zuni Folk Tales* (1931). General Collections.

From the beginning of European settlement in America, children have been exposed to the printed word. Often this took a unique shape—hornbooks, chapbooks, primers, little Bibles—but the purpose was the same for all: to rigorously teach reading. Between 1683 and 1776, *The New-England Primer* was the only schoolbook used, a position of influence supplanted after 1836 by *The McGuffey Reader*. *The Eclectic Readers* of William McGuffey (1800-1873) combined literary lessons, moral teaching, and selections from great writers. Most of these writers were English, which—due to the fact that McGuffey's *Readers* sold over 125 million copies in 200 separate editions—profoundly shaped American cultural attitudes in the nineteenth century.

Once these texts set the foundation, American children were able to enjoy and explore the new worlds open to them. Uniquely American characters populated this world: from American Indian folktales, African-American fables, *Peter Parley*, *Cock Robin*, and *Mother Goose* nursery rhymes for the youngest to motivational novels of Horatio Alger, Jr., tales of manners by Louisa May Alcott, and the fantasy lands of Oz and Sleepy Hollow for juvenile readers. The Library of Congress has over 200,000 children's books in its collections and, in 1963, established a Children's Literature Center.

Mother Goose was "pirated" from the British original in 1780. This expanded, Americanized edition was published in 1833. Rare Book and Special Collections Division.

Illustration from the title page of *McGuffey's Third Eclectic Reader*. General Collections.

Tales For Children

The units presented here are reprints of two of the 16 panels that comprise the "Books That Shaped America" display, which was written and compiled by Alan Bisbort and designed by Eddins, Madison & Spitz of Alexandria, Virginia.

For more information about the Library of Congress Corner series, contact SIRS, Inc., P.O. Box 2348, Boca Raton, FL 33427-2348, 1-800-232-SIRS.

A CENTER FOR THE BOOK

In 1977, our nation's love of books was embraced by the law of the land when the Center for the Book was established. Public Law 95-129, passed by Congress and signed by President Carter, created the Center for the Book to "stimulate public interest and research in the role of the book in the diffusion of knowledge," as well as to promote a nation-wide interest in books and reading. Its activities include reading promotion projects (Read More About It, Books Make a Difference, Books Change Lives), symposia, lectures, exhibitions, and, of course, the publication of books. Since 1984, the Center's efforts "to keep the book flourishing" have been helped immeasurably by the creation of 29 state or regional affiliates around the country. These centers help make certain that books will continue to shape America.

The Misty books, set on coastal Virginia's Chincoteague Island, have always been a favorite of those who dream of owning a pony. Center for the Book.

The Reader
BY WILL BARNET

Inspired by fond childhood memories of his Massachusetts town's public library—and the haven it provided him after World War I—the great American artist Will Barnet created this poster, "The Reader," in 1979. With the artist's permission, the Center for the Book has adopted the work, using "The Reader" to illustrate its many outreach programs. Center for the Book.

READ MORE ABOUT IT:

Bailyn, Bernard. *The Ideological Origins of the American Revolution*. Cambridge: Harvard Press, 1967.

Cole, John Y. *Jefferson's Legacy*. Washington: LC, 1993.

Downs, Robert B. *Books That Changed the World*. Chicago: American Library Association, 1978.

Padover, Saul. *The Living U.S. Constitution*. New York: NAL, 1987.

Rutland, Robert A. *Well Acquainted with Books: The Founding Framers of 1787*. Washington: LC, 1987.

CREDITS:

"Books That Shaped America" was written and compiled by Alan Bisbort, Library of Congress Publishing Office. Designed by Eddins, Madison & Spitz, Alexandria, VA. Published and distributed by SIRS (Social Issues Resources Series) Inc., P.O. Box 2348, Boca Raton, FL 33427.

Still Shaping

SIRS Library of Congress Corner

BOOKS THAT SHAPED AMERICA — UNIT 16

L E T T E R S

THE APRIL-MAY 1993 ISSUE OF READING TODAY, BIMONTHLY NEWSPAPER OF

THE INTERNATIONAL READING ASSOCIATION, CARRIED A LETTER FROM A

READER, GUADELUPE CRUZ, ON THE POWERFUL INFLUENCE OF READING

BOOKS ON HIS LIFE, AND IN AN ACCOMPANYING ARTICLE ASKED READERS,

"HAVE BOOKS REALLY CHANGED YOUR LIFE? HAVE THEY MADE YOU LAUGH

OR CRY? HELPED YOU OVERCOME A PERSONAL CRISIS? LED YOU TO YOUR CA-

REER? BROUGHT ABOUT A SPIRITUAL OR INTELLECTUAL REVELATION?" IT

THEN INVITED THEM TO SUBMIT BRIEF LETTERS, 250 WORDS OR FEWER, THAT

DESCRIBE HOW BOOKS HAVE CHANGED THEIR LIVES. FOLLOWING IS MR.

CRUZ'S LETTER AND A SELECTION OF RESPONSES FROM READERS, DRAWN

FROM THE DECEMBER 1993 / JANUARY 1994, JUNE / JULY 1994, AND

DECEMBER 1994 / JANUARY 1995 ISSUES OF READING TODAY.

My name is Guadelupe Cruz, and I'm 29 years of age. I've been reading ever since I was a small child, but I never enjoyed reading until a couple of years ago when I went to Mexico City on a bus. I lived in Garden City, Kansas, and by the time we got to Oklahoma City I was extremely bored.

During my layover there, I walked across the street to a secondhand shop. While I was there, I came upon many used books. I wasn't able to look at them all, but I purchased three of them—*Of Mice and Men* by John Steinbeck, *The Hound of the Baskervilles* by Sir Arthur Conan Doyle, and *Anne Frank: The Diary of A Young Girl* by Anne Frank.

Well, since then I no longer enjoy television except for PBS programs and the news. Reading has now become a major part of my daily life, and I now have a private library with over 200 books. My favorite fiction includes: *Lord of the Flies* by William Golding, *Ship of Fools* by Katherine Anne Porter, *The Grapes of Wrath*, by John Steinbeck, *Hamlet, The Merchant of Venice, Romeo and Juliet, Macbeth*, and *Julius Caesar* by William Shapespeare, *All the King's Men* by Robert Penn Warren, *The Scarlet Letter* by Nathaniel Hawthorne, *The Rainbow* by D.H. Lawrence, and *Clear and Present Danger* and *The Hunt for Red October* by Tom Clancy.

My nonfiction collection includes *Holocaust: The History of the Jews of Europe During the Second World War* by Martin Gilbert, *Born Free* by Joy Adamson, *Death Be Not Proud* by John Gunther, and *Breaking Point* by Jack and Joann Hinckley.

As can be seen, I truly enjoy reading. I hope to continue adding on to my library. However, most of my books are used. I can't believe that so many people do away with their books. Some people donate them to secondhand shops, but I wonder how many are thrown away.

Guadelupe Cruz
Deerfield, Kansas

The Red Badge of Courage, by Stephen Crane—I can't say the title without once again being a young girl in seventh grade hanging on every word that came from my teacher's mouth as she read aloud to me the first real classic I had ever heard.

Back then, reading aloud to older students was considered a waste of valuable time. Yet every afternoon during that glorious month when we studied the Civil War, Mrs. Ducas would close the classroom door and make the pain and the glory, the loss and the greatness, the struggle and the victory of that time in history come alive.

Hearing *The Red Badge of Courage* remains one of the fondest and most poignant memories of my education. It began my love of reading, it is the basis for my passion about Civil War history, and it directed me to the profession of education.

As a teacher I try not to let a day pass without reading aloud to my own students. I often look at their young faces and wonder which marvelous tale, intriguing mystery, or heartfelt saga will be the story that will change their lives.

Karen J. Durica
Littleton, Colorado

———————⟨📖⟩———————

Nearly four decades have passed since the book first appeared on my bedroom pillow for my 19th birthday. Home on leave from the Marines, my dad left the book with a brief note written in his peculiar left-handed scrawl.

"I think you'll enjoy this, Son," he wrote. "Read and reread this."

I have. But I came to it slowly. *This Hallowed Ground*, Bruce Catton's poetic rendering of the American Civil War, lay in the bottom of my Marine footlocker for two years. When I returned to college, its white and black cover dulled in the sunlight on a ledge near a dormitory window. Then, one night, faced with the need for a report on a book, any book, I broke the seal and entered a lifetime of entertainment and instruction.

I completed the book report but found myself reading and rereading Catton's epic work just as Dad had instructed. I marched with Grant's Union Sixth Corps on the muddy roads within the wilderness in the mo-

ments during the spring of 1864 before the Confederates struck as one along the Orange Plank Road. I followed Lee and his men north across the Potomac, the water soiled red from the cuts inflicted by a thousand stone on thousands of bleeding southern feet. I stood at Appomattox as the Army of Northern Virginia at last dipped its flags in defeat. There, the battle streamers outnumbered the Confederate veterans who remained.

Perhaps naturally, the epic grandeur of *This Hallowed Ground* nudged me into my own Army of Northern Virginia. And in 1966, I, like many of my Marine comrades found myself turning in my few civilian possessions for storage at the San Diego USO.

"They'll be here when you return, Sergeant," a bright-eyed volunteer told me. Thirteen months later, the same lady apologized. "Your two pairs of shirts and pants are gone, Sergeant. But we can let you pick from the clothes that won't be picked up."

I declined and asked about my package.

"Yes, we have that," she brightened.

And so once again I had *This Hallowed Ground*. On my next Vietnam tour, it went with me, stuffed in the bottom of my pack and often left in base camp. The moisture molded the cover and the red dust ravaged the pages. But Catton's easy cadences continued to grip my interest even in a place that mirrored the travail of the Civil War's Cold Harbor and Spotsylvania.

Home, *This Hallowed Ground* followed me through long months at Balboa Naval Hospital and subsequently back to school. Later, writing my dissertation, I turned every morning to again dip a fly into the clear bottomless pools of Catton's prose, finding new truth and additional inspiration in waters yet unfished.

Now the tattered old volume rests next to my reading chair. Like the man who holds and reflects upon it daily, time has marked and changed the volume. The hard cover has grown soft, the once pristine pages now appear soiled and wrinkled. And yet, mysteries and inspiration still renew the reader in the optimism and beauty that journalist Bruce Catton found in the most epic of American tragedies, the Civil War

And still taped on the back cover of Catton's work remains Dad's wise directive on my 19th birthday.

"I think you'll enjoy this, Son. Read and reread this."

I have, Dad.

Mike Fisher
Tucson, Arizona

I am an ardent reader, a reading teacher, a reading mom, and a graduate student in reading. It all began in a place I still remember the look of, the smell of, and the feeling of—the children's room of a small public library in Norristown, Pennsylvania.

It was the late 1950s, and I was a second-grade child looking for something to read. (This was before the proliferation of children's books in homes—at least in my home and those of my friends.) My parochial school had neither classroom nor building libraries.

Walking into the library, I can recall seeing so many books there and wanting to read every one. Over the years, the small library card with its metal strip identification number became ink-stained with use. I did read each picture book in the library and moved on to chapter books. Suddenly I was bringing home biographies of Douglas MacArthur and Gandhi.

I read with delight then and now, not realizing until now how profoundly books changed my life almost as soon as I could read.

Judy Grumet
Pittsburgh, Pennsylvania

It was a time before television, before affluence. For me, it was even before kindergarten. What was a lonely only child to do? I learned to read.

The story was *The Three Bears*. Since I knew the title and had memorized the opening "Once upon a time..." I already had a reading vocabulary of seven words. "What does t-h-e-r-e spell?" I asked. It was early morning and every adult was still sleeping, or trying to. I tugged gently on a pajama sleeve. "What does w-e-r-e spell?" I asked. Now I had nine words! So it went, and I haven't stopped reading since.

As a slightly older child, I fell in love with *Little Women*. Of course I searched for other books by Louisa May Alcott. In my rural school library I found *Rose in Bloom* and eagerly took it to the fifth-grader who was checking out books. "You can't read that," she said. (Although I was in third grade, I was only seven and small for my age.) She actually meant

to not let me have it. Normally shy, I drew myself to my full height and said bravely, "But I've read all her other books!" She let me sign it out.

That winter I got rheumatic fever. The doctor ordered me to remain in bed and not to walk at all. Each day my mother would stop at a second-hand bookstore on her way home from work and bring me more books. They became my life and my lifeline. Books made a winter of illness a truly happy one.

As a high-schooler in a small city, I visited the main library almost daily. It was a gracious building with marble floors and dark wood shelves. Its central reading room held thousands of volumes. My mother recalls that I came home from the library one day depressed and on the verge of tears because I had just realized that no matter how fast and how much I read I could never read every book in that library, much less in the world.

That didn't stop me, though. In college, *The Plague* by Albert Camus, was assigned reading. The issues that it raised of good and evil and responsibility for one's own behavior impressed me deeply at the time. I have continued to think deeply and long about these subjects, and I have reread The Plague often.

The most influential professional book for me was also one I first read in college. I was an art education major and Viktor Lowenfeld's *Creative and Mental Growth* was our bible. Like all great books, it was not just about its specific subject. Rather, it was about all education; it was about life.

Thomas Jefferson could have been speaking for me when he said, "I cannot live without books."

May Kanfer
Bronxville, New York

Yes, books have really changed my life, to the better. They have directed me to being an open-minded person, tolerant of other cultures, tolerant of other people, of their thoughts, their beliefs, and of their behavior.

I was 10 years old when I first read—in Turkish translation—Tolstoy's *War and Peace*. I did not have any grown-ups around me to guide me as to what—and how—I should read. My classmates were not very much into reading. Even those who did like reading did not choose to—or did not have the chance to—read such thick books anyway. So, I was Alice—alone—in the Wonderland of books.

War and Peace, of course, was but a long story to a 10-year-old without grown-ups' guidance. I did not realize then that I was reading a very famous book, a highly respected account of an important part of the Russian history. Still, one does not need much guidance to enjoy reading, nor does one need to know one is reading a well-known book.

I can still see—very vividly, too—Natasha hurriedly getting ready for her debutante party. And Andrei, lying injured in the battlefield, under the blazing sun.

I probably don't remember all this from that first reading, I read the book many times over the years. Each time I enjoyed reading it, and each time I found new things in it. When I was 12 or so, they put *War and Peace* on television as a series. Natasha looked so much like the Natasha I had been imagining. But there was something missing in the TV series: the intimacy I had with those characters in the book.

I studied English literature at the university, and I learned to read beyond the story, with a critical eye. When I had to read *Anna Karenina* in a world literature elective, and analyze the characters' psychology, etc., I found it easy to comment on the Russian side of things. After reading several books by Tolstoy, Gorki, and Pushkin, without knowing it, I had come to have some familiarity with the Russians—as portrayed in these books, of course. I had a sense of what it was like to live in such a cold climate, as opposed to the Mediterranean warmth I grew up in.

Today I am an English teacher. I teach my students to look at and describe the world in a foreign language. I try to help them get out of the boundaries of their mother tongue, and look at language, and life in general, in a more flexible way, more aware of the need to adapt themselves to things, rather than blindly resist changes brought by new things.

I still read just for pleasure. I still have not lost the ability to really enjoy reading a book. I still have the ability to pick up things from a book while reading and enjoying it, instead of reading it to find things for criticism purposes only, although I should also admit that the critical eye I acquired has made me a more aware reader.

I have been to, and lived in, several foreign countries. But no visit or stay has been as pleasurable and meaningful as those I had, and still have, when I read a book and find myself visiting another country, another culture. Through books, I have been to India with British colonizers, and to London with a middle-aged English actress. I have been to the New York of the 1920s with a Greek immigrant who was born in Turkey. Through books I have been to many places around the world, each time as a different person from a different background.

So, when I look at the world, it is not just from a narrow window now. My view is not limited (at least not limited too much, I hope) by my nationality, my native language, my formal educational background, etc. The least I can say for sure is that I have at times looked at the world through another's eyes, and this has made me a better person.

Selda Sönmez Mansour
Famagust, North Cyprus

I grew up as an African-American female child in a rural, culturally deprived area of East Texas. As such, I was largely unexposed to many of the same rights and privileges as my white contemporaries, even though both of my parents were college-educated teachers who worked in the school system.

By the time my hometown was court-ordered to desegregate the schools, I had completed two years at the Negro campus. Once I got to the "new" school, my teacher recommended me for remedial reading. By their measure, I was considered to be what we now term "at risk." My mother was a reading specialist, and she worked with me at home.

I learned to dislike reading books from an early age because I felt unsuccessful. My reading was slow and laborious. I seldom got meaning from what I read because of the effort I spent on fluency. I often reread for meaning. I later learned that was all right to do.

I went through my primary years of school and some secondary years before having a teacher who really turned me on to books. Then I started combing the bookstores and libraries for titles about children who had things in common with me. While taking children's literature courses in college, I received a wealth of knowledge about good children's books, and I read them with a passion.

My bittersweet experiences with books molded me into a multifaceted teacher, a conscientious mother, and a published writer. I wouldn't take anything from my journey now.

Cahndice S. Matthews
San Antonio, Texas

At the age of 20, a year after I had dropped out of college, I was diagnosed with a brain tumor. Five months later, on January 21, 1985, the doctors successfully removed the tumor. I immediately began a rehabilitation program consisting of low-impact exercise, tutoring in the language arts, and psychotherapy for head trauma cases.

By the end of the spring, I decided with the help of my parents, brothers, and tutor, that I needed to return to school. I enrolled in a small college in Florida and planned to begin classes the following spring semester. In the meantime, I planned to spend the summer working at the New Jersey shore with a good friend, as I had done in the past. In the fall I would begin being tutored again to prepare for school.

During the summer months I didn't want to socialize much. My roommate, a friend since I was six years old, seemed to know when to leave me alone and when to drag me out of our small apartment to a club or a party.

Since I worked nights in a club, I often spent my days walking along the beach, boardwalk, and streets of the summer resort, lost in thought. One day as I was walking down the main avenue of the island I found myself standing in front of a bookstore. Deciding that I could use something to read on the beach (my reading material was usually the latest issue of *Sports Illustrated*), I went inside.

For some unknown reason, I elected to pass by the magazine rack and wander through the shelves of books. I hadn't the faintest idea what I was looking for. I had never read books for pleasure in the past, but I knew I wanted to read more than an article on the latest hot college basketball recruit or predictions for the upcoming NFL season.

As I scanned a rack of books, a small ruddy-colored paperback caught my eye. It was J.D. Salinger's *The Catcher in the Rye*. I recalled having read some of it while in junior high. As I held the book, I remembered that my teacher had told us to reread it when we were older, so I purchased it.

That evening when I began reading it, I immediately felt a connection with Holden Caulfield. I couldn't put the book down and took it with me to work. In the smoke-filled club, amid flashing lights, pounding music, intoxicated dances, and demands for drinks, I leaned against the bar reading.

The next day I closed the book, sorry that it had ended. What an experience! I quickly ran to the store and bought another book. I devoured everything by Salinger and then moved on to other writers. I was hooked.

I went on to school and graduated with an English degree from St. Joseph's University. I am currently enrolled at Rider University, where I am a candidate for a master's degree in their reading/language arts program. I can't imagine where I would be today if not for books.

David Morgan
Warrington, Pennsylvania

My lifelong pursuit of learning is tied to a steady and hungry pursuit of good literature. As a child I watched my father read. His appetite for books was insatiable, and he read with evident pleasure. He would smile and murmur his favorite lines, twisting in his chair with excitement, and sometimes even laughing out loud.

My mother read aloud to my brother and me from the Bible and a wonderfully illustrated book of Robert Louis Stevenson's *A Child's Garden of Verses*. She took us faithfully to the public library, where we learned the smell and feel of books and came to know that the knowledge within those pages was meant for us.

Currently I read over 100 books a year. Natural history, the classics, and books on Abraham Lincoln comprise the bulk of my reading. My favorites include the complete nature writings of John Burroughs, *Pilgrim at Tinker Creek* by Annie Dillard, *The Mountains* by Stewart Edward White, *Abraham Lincoln* by Benjamin Thomas, the Bible, and *Don Quixote* by Cervantes.

People often complain that they have no time to read. As a parent and a full-time primary grade teacher, I still manage to make time for reading. I read late in the evening, early in the morning, and whenever I have to wait for someone. I also choose to read rather than watch television. For me, reading is as natural as breathing, and as necessary.

Victoria Perry
Cornish, Maine

In the fall of 1952, as Jonas Salk was busy developing his polio vaccine, my seven-year-old body was busy developing a case of polio. Luckily, a first floor bedroom, a mom home full time, and a caring doctor allowed me to avoid the hospital.

Being flat on my back for six weeks limited my options for overcoming boredom. We didn't have a TV, and I could only listen to so much Arthur Godfrey and "Stella Dallas" on the radio Dad installed on a shelf in the built-in bunkbed. The same shelf was long enough to hold several books.

Being several weeks into second grade, I was reading fairly fluently.

In that bedroom I read my first "chapter" book, *The Happy Hollisters*. I lived in *The Little House in the Big Woods* and followed as best I could the adventures of *Big Red*. For those six weeks, reading was my only transportation out of that bed and room.

Today reading is still the escape valve, the stress reducer, the refuge, the dream stimulator, and the avenue to anything I need—*The Bridges of Madison County* to serve romantic whims, *The Art of Meditation* for solace, and *Horace's Compromise* to enrich my thinking about school transformation.

Carol Reinhard
Des Moines, Iowa

BOOKS CHANGE LIVES

1993-1994
National Campaign Report

PART TWO

Attorney General Janet Reno, Senator Paul Simon (center) and Reading Rainbow host LaVar Burton (right) celebrate "Books Change Lives" at the Library of Congress in September 1993.

Author Sidney Sheldon looks at his own comments about the value of libraries in the "Libraries Change Lives" travelling exhibition sponsored by the American Library Association.

A young Head Start student adds to a "reading mural" during the Center for the Book's celebration of International Literacy Day on Sept. 8, 1994.

1993

All year

The Department of Defense Dependents' school system uses the "Books Change Lives" (BCL) theme in its Director's "Challenge of Reading" and other reading activities in some 200 schools serving U.S. military and other U.S. government dependents in 19 countries around the world.

January 28

Representatives of more than 40 organizations enrolled as Reading Promotion Partners of the Library of Congress meet at the Library to review activities undertaken during the 1992 campaign, "Explore New Worlds—READ!," and to discuss plans for the two-year BCL campaign that had begun on New Year's Day.

April 19

Representatives from more than 25 state centers meet at the Library of Congress for the annual State Center Day, to exchange ideas on effective individual programs and consider future activities related to the BCL campaign.

September

The Center for the Book notifies the state centers that up to 12 of them would be able to participate in a forthcoming national student "Letters About Literature" contest on the BCL theme, to be announced by *Read* magazine in November. State centers taking part would help publicize the contest and, in the spring of 1994, help select the winner in their respective states. Each state winner would receive a cash award of $100, to be presented by his or her state center. The national winner would receive an all-expenses paid trip to Washington, D.C., and a visit to the Library of Congress.

October 23

The U.S. Postal Service issues a poster, "Curl Up With A Good Stamp," later placed on display in the 9,000 largest post offices in the country, honoring four new 29-cent stamps featuring classic children's books, *Little Women* by Louisa May Alcott, *The Adventures of Huckleberry Finn* by Mark Twain, *Rebecca of Sunnybrook Farm* by Kate Douglas Wiggin, and *Little House on the Prairie* by Laura Ingalls Wilder. Carrying the legend, "Discover the wonderful worlds of reading books and saving stamps," the poster displays both the logo of the Postal Service and that of the Center for the Book, with "Books Change Lives" in the place of "Books Give Us Wings." Invited to Nashville by the Postal Service, John Y. Cole, director of the center, speaks on behalf of the Center for the Book about the BCL campaign at ceremonies marking the first day of issue.

1994

All year
The U.S. Department of Defense Dependents' school system once again uses the BCL theme in its Director's "Challenge of Reading" and other reading activities.

January 19
Hardy representatives of 15 of the Reading Promotion Partners, along with a courageous observer from the American College of Physicians, who travelled down from Philadelphia by train, meet at the James Madison Memorial Building of the Library of Congress. Despite a snowstorm and near record cold for the annual partners' "Idea Exchange," they review activities during the first year of the BCL campaign and discuss possibilities for the final months ahead. Learning of the Correctional Education Association's 1993 essay contest on the BCL theme for inmates, the editor of the International Reading Association's biweekly newspaper, *Reading Today*, arranged to receive a copy of the text, when it became available, for reprinting in his paper.

March 10
The Center for the Book and the National Newspaper Foundation co-sponsor a lunch at the Library of Congress for members of the National Newspaper Association. This professional association, representing the interests of more than 4,600 community newspapers, was in town attending the 33rd annual Congressional Affairs Conference. In their remarks during the lunch, Librarian of Congress James H. Billington and Center for the Book director John Cole each make the point that reading newspapers, too, changes lives.

April 17-23
The theme of National Library Week, chosen by the American Library Association, is a variation on BCL, "Libraries Change Lives."

April 18
Representatives from more than 25 state centers for the book meet at the Library of Congress for the annual State Center Day, in which state center contributions to the BCL campaign are shared.

April 18
Twelfth-grader Aslum Khan, of Rolling Meadows, Illinois, national winner of *Read* magazine's first national "Letters About Literature" campaign, visits the Library of Congress with his family and talks to state center representatives about his winning essay (see page 18).

September
The Center for the Book distributes the first issue of *Partner's Update*, a newsletter for Reading Promotion Partners of the Library of Congress that provides information on partner activities related to the campaign.

September 8
To celebrate International Literacy Day, the Center for the Book makes it possible for Cartoonists Across America (CAA) to complete the world's largest literacy mural in front of the James Madison Memorial Building of the Library of Congress, by adding the BCL theme to both sides of a 53-foot truck trailer donated by the Jones Motor Group of Spring City, Pennsylvania. The truck arrives in front of the Madison Building shortly after 8 a.m. and remains all day. While some CAA artists add new details to the mural, others direct children from a District of Columbia Head Start program and eager passersby in adding fresh paint to parts of the mural that have faded from exposure to the weather. The truck is to continue on the road for the next five years, carrying its multiple messages on the importance of literacy and reading to every corner of the continental U.S.

October 26
The Center for the Book hosts an awards ceremony and reception at the James Madison Memorial Building for the Board of Directors of the Women's National Book Association, honoring the 1994 WNBA Award recipient, Janet Palmer Mullaney, editor and publisher of *Belles Lettres: A Review of Books by Women*. John Cole, in introductory remarks, explains the relevance of the event to the BCL campaign.

Alaska

The Alaska Center for the Book distributed BCL brochures throughout 1993 and 1994.

California

The California Center for the Book distributed BCL brochures at a reading promotion event in Sacramento, "Sacramento Reads!"; at the California Literacy Conference, also in Sacramento, in September 1993; at the San Francisco Bay Area Book Festival, in October 1993; and at the California Library Association meeting, in Long Beach, in November 1993.

Colorado

During National Library Week in April, 1993, the Colorado Center for the Book used the BCL theme in information packets on the promotion of literacy and reading and the use of libraries sent to 1,000 Colorado libraries. It also used the theme to publicize ACCESS, the new electronic network that links users to the data base of all Colorado library holdings. In 1994, a thousand elementary and high school students throughout Colorado submitted entries to a poster contest for the 1994 Rocky Mountain Book Festival, sponsored by the Colorado Center for the Book. Students in grades K-12 were asked to create a poster with the words "Libraries Change Lives, Books Change Lives." The grand prize winner, Josh Aho, a student at Thompson Valley High School in Loveland, received a $100 gift certificate to Walden Books in Fort Collins. His art teacher, Joy Shaw, received a $250 gift certificate for her school to be used at the Tattered Cover Bookshop in Denver. Schools and libraries displayed the poster to promote the book festival. The Colorado Center for the Book served as state co-sponsor for *Read* magazine's 1994-1995 "Letters About Literature" contest, which used BCL as the theme on which the contestants had to write. The Center helped select the state winner, to whom the center awarded a prize of $100.

Connecticut

The Connecticut Center for the Book served as state co-sponsor for *Read* magazine's 1993-1994 national "Letters About Literature" contest on the BCL theme, helping to select the state winner, to whom the center awarded a prize of $100.

Delaware

The Westminster Presbyterian Church, in Wilmington, displayed BCL posters and brochures at the reopening of its library, after extensive renovation and expansion, in April 1994.

Florida

The Florida Center for the Book served as state co-sponsor for *Read* magazine's 1993-1994 and 1994-1995 national "Letters About Literature" contests using the BCL theme. The Center helped select the state winners each time, to whom it awarded a prize of $100. At the request of the Florida center, Librarian of Congress James H. Billington—visiting Fort Lauderdale on April 21, 1994, to open the Library of Congress's travelling exhibit on literary America, "The Language of the Land"—gave the prize for the Florida state winner of the 1993-1994 "Letters About Literature" contest to Natasha Gaziano for her letter about *The Diary of a Young Girl*, by Anne Frank (see page 15).

Illinois

The March 1994 issue of *ICB Anthology*, newsletter of the Illinois Center for the Book, carried a front page article on Aslum Khan, the Illinois high school student who won Read magazine's 1993-94 "Letters About Literature" contest. The contest, co-sponsored by the Illinois Center, was open to high school students, each of whom were asked to write an essay about a book that had changed his or her life. *ICB Anthology* board member Susan Sussman was one of four judges to select three state winners from the submissions of some 4,000 Illinois participants, almost half of the 9,000 entries submitted from all over the country. The newsletter also carried a profile of Aslum Khan in a separate box on the front page. The Illinois Center for the Book also participated in *Read* magazine's "Letters About Literature" contest for 1994-1995, which once again used the BCL theme.

Iowa

In September 1993, the Iowa Center for the Book decorated the Des Moines Public Library with "Books Change Lives" and "How Libraries Change Lives" window displays to publicize a display of posters announcing the seventh annual "LAGBRAI" (Libraries Annual Great Book Read Across Iowa), a center-sponsored event. The center also used "How Libraries Change Lives" on posters publicizing LAGBRAI VII. The Iowa center was also a state co-sponsor for *Read* magazine's "Letters About Literature" contest on the BCL theme, in 1993-1994 and again in 1994-1995, each time helping to select the state winner, to whom it awarded a prize of $100.

Kansas

In April 1994, author Jean Auel, her conference tour sponsored by the Kansas Center for the Book and funded by the National Book Foundation and the Lila Wallace-Reader's Digest Fund, spoke to standing-room-only audiences in Olathe, Lawrence, and Topeka. At each event, she used "Books Change Lives" and "Libraries Change Lives" as the theme of her remarks. Her audiences included aspiring students of writing at Washburn University in Topeka and academics in the fields of sociology, anthropology, and paleontology at Kansas University. On October 14-15, 1994, the Kansas Center for the Book sponsored the third Kansas Young Readers' Conference. Held at Fort Hays State University, in Hays, Kansas, the two-day conference—attended by 750 children, grades 3 through 6—was intended to give children, primarily from rural school districts, a chance to understand how books change lives, to meet famous authors and illustrators and to encourage both the reading of good books and the growth of aspiring young writers and illustrators. It was also hoped that this would enhance school curricula by introducing books and, through them, issues to teachers and parents that they might otherwise not have come to know.

The effects of the 1993-1994 BCL campaign were still being felt on April 6, 1995, when Governor William Graves of Kansas, acting on a petition from the Kansas Library Association, the Director of the Topeka & Shawnee County Public Library, and the Kansas Center for the Book, signed a proclamation designating October as Library Month in Kansas. His action made it possible for the Kansas Center for the Book to start work on a traveling display and brochure featuring pictures of famous Kansans and their statements on how books and libraries changed their lives.

Michigan

February 1993, "Books Change Lives" (BCL) was the theme for National Book Week at the Library of Michigan, in Lansing, while a variant, "Libraries Change Lives," was used as the theme for National Library Week, celebrated April 18-24, 1993, and April 17-23, 1994. The events were covered in *Access*, the Library of Michigan's bimonthly newsletter, for March-April 1993. At the 1993 Michigan Festival, held August 6-15 on the campus of Michigan State University, Michigan Center for the Book personnel promoted the "Books Change Lives" theme and distributed approximately 8,000 BCL buttons. Library of Michigan staff members wore "Books Change Lives" T-shirts when they volunteered on two weekends (August 6 and 15) to represent the center, which had display space assigned. The issue of *Access* for November-December 1993, reproduced a photograph of members of the board of directors of the Michigan Center for the Book "show[ing] off the colorful "Books Change Lives" tee-shirts received at a recent meeting in Lansing." The Michigan Center for the Book acted as co-sponsor for the state of Michigan of both *Read* magazine's 1993-1994 and 1994-1995 "Letters About Literature" contests on the BCL theme, helping each time to select the state winner, to whom it awarded a prize of $100.

Minnesota

The Minnesota Center for the Book placed the BCL theme prominently in publicity related to Minnesota's "Week in Winter" celebrations (traditionally coinciding with National Book Week in January) both in 1993 and 1994. These celebrations, which focus on the importance of books, reading, authors, and libraries, are co-sponsored by libraries and booksellers across the state. In 1993, the "Week in Winter" attracted unusual attention when the Minnesota center, sponsored a talk at the University of St. Thomas, in Saint Paul, by author Barry Lopez, winner of the National Book Award for *Arctic Dreams*. In 1994, the second year of the campaign, the economic importance of the "Week in Winter" helped garner financial support from the Minnesota Department of Trade and Economic Development. On April 23, 1993, Justice Rosalie Wahl gave the keynote address, on the theme "Books Change Lives," at the fifth annual presentation of the Minnesota Book Awards, sponsored by the Minnesota Center for the Book, together with Partners in the Minnesota Community of the Book, at the Minnesota History Center in Saint Paul. In its April 1994 newsletter the Mount Olive Lutheran Church library informed parishioners that the BCL variation, "Libraries Change Lives," was the theme of National Library Week (April 17-23) and enquired of its readers, "How have libraries changed your lives?" The Minnesota Center for the Book served as co-sponsor for the state of Minnesota for *Read* magazine's 1993-1994 and 1994-1995 "Letters About Literature" contests on the BCL theme, helping to select the state winner, to whom it awarded a prize of $100.

Missouri

The January-February 1993 issue of *Missouri Libraries*, bimonthly publication of the Missouri State Library, proclaimed BCL as the Library of Congress's reading theme for 1993-1994 and offered suggestions on how to promote the theme. The July-August 1994 issue of *Missouri Libraries* announced that the Missouri Center for the Book would serve as co-sponsor for the state of Missouri of the 1994-1995 *Read* magazine "Letters About Literature" contest on the theme "Books Change Lives," helping to select the state winner, to whom it awarded a prize of $100.

Nebraska

On April 22, 1994, Morrill Elementary School, in Mitchell, held a Read-A-Thon in which a student earned one "Morrill Buck" for each 20 minutes of personal reading and then could use his earnings to acquire items donated to the school. Reporting on the event, the local *Mitchell Index* showed one young reader, Chris Wetherington, proudly wearing the BCL sweatshirt, with Thomas Jefferson's "I cannot live without books" emblazoned across the front, and a BCL brochure in his hand.

New Jersey

Throughout 1993 and 1994, the New Jersey Connection energetically propagated the BCL theme, introducing a variation during the second year of the campaign: "Reading Changes Lives." The theme appeared in the New Jersey Connection's letterhead, in announcements of its annual New Jersey Enthusiastic Reader Awards and newly introduced New Jersey Enthusiastic Librarian or Teacher Award, in announcements of readathons, on posters publicizing the recipients of the annual Enthusiastic Reader Awards, and on the cover of New Jersey Connection publications, like its annual *A Book of New Jersey Students' Writing About Reading*, a collection of writings about reading by students in New Jersey schools. On May 13, 1994, during a ceremony at Monmouth College in which the annual New Jersey Enthusiastic Reader Awards were being made, a representative of Governor Christine Whitman announced that the governor had issued a proclamation stating that BCL was the state reading theme for 1994. (For more details, see under **New Jersey Connection**, in the **NATIONAL ASSOCIATIONS AND ORGANIZATIONS** on page 57.)

New York

In November 1993, the New York chapter of the Women's National Book Association organized its program meeting around the BCL theme.

North Dakota

The North Dakota Center for the Book served as co-sponsor of the state's *Read* magazine's 1993-1994 and 1994-1995 "Letters About Literature" contests on the BCL theme, helping select the state winner, to whom it awarded a prize of $100.

Ohio

The Ohio Center for the Book served as co-sponsor of the state's *Read* magazine's 1993-1994 and 1994-1995 "Letters About Literature" contest on the BCL theme, helping select the state winner, to whom it awarded a prize of $100.

Oregon

The Oregon Center for the Book served as co-sponsor of the state's Weekly Reader Corporation's *Read* magazine's "Letters About Literature" in 1994-1995 and awarded the state winner a prize of $100.

Pennsylvania

On March 17, 1993, the Speaker of the Pennsylvania House of Representatives informed the members by memorandum (Subject: "Books Change Lives") that each of them should submit to him by April 15 the name of a book that had changed their life. (His own choice was the dictionary.) On March 18, Governor Robert P. Casey proclaimed May 1993 "Books Change Lives" Month, following the introduction in the Pennsylvania House of Representatives that same day of a resolution by the Speaker to the same effect. Also in 1993, Borders Book Shops in Philadelphia, Lancaster, and Pittsburgh announced a Books Change Lives writing contest co-sponsored by Pizza Hut and the Pennsylvania Center for the Book, with entries—either an essay or a poem, on the theme of a book or author who has changed the writer's life—to be submitted to Borders Book Shops during National Library Week. Winner of the 1st prize received a certificate from Governor and Mrs. Casey, a book from Borders Book Shop, and a certificate from Pizza Hut for a class pizza party. Winners of the 2nd and 3rd prizes each received a copy of the proclamation from Governor Casey and a book from Borders Book Shop.

On May 26, the House recognized the winning students and the importance of books by suspending session to allow the students to come onto the floor and meet with their representatives. Immediately thereafter, the House went into recess so that members could attend a pizza party for the students in the East Wing of the capitol, sponsored by Pizza Hut.

Tennessee

In August 1992, the Nashville chapter of the Women's National Book Association used the BCL theme to decorate a combined informative brochure and membership application form. On March 19-20, 1993, the Kingsport, chapter of the American Association of University Women held a booksale, at which it issued bookmarks decorated with the Center for the Book's "Books Give Us Wings" logo. On July 25, 1994, the newspaper-in-education coordinator for the *Kingsport Times-News* held a teacher workshop at which she distributed 150 BCL brochures.

Texas

The Texas Center for the Book participated, as a co-sponsor for the state of Texas, in *Read* magazine's 1994-1995 essay contest on the theme BCL, giving the state winner a $100 prize.

Virginia

The Virginia Center for the Book served as a co-sponsor for the state of Virginia of both *Read* magazine's 1993-1994 and 1994-1995 "Letters About Literature" contests on the BCL theme, helping each time to select the state winner, to whom it awarded a prize of $100.

Washington

In honor of National Book Week, January 18-23, 1993, the Washington Center for the Book and the Seattle Public Library issued bookmarks in a variety of colors decorated with the "Books Change Lives" logo and listing the three National Book Award winners, one each for fiction, non-fiction, and poetry.

Wisconsin

The Wisconsin Center for the Book served as a state co-sponsor of both *Read* magazine's 1994 and 1994-1995 "Letters About Literature" contests on the BCL theme, helping to select each of the state winners, to whom it awarded a prize of $100.

The fall 1992 issue of LCLA *Chapter Open Mike*, quarterly newsletter of the Lutheran Church Library Association, was the first publication to announce BCL as the reading promotion theme of the Library of Congress for 1993-1994.

The October-November 1992 issue of *Reading Today*, biweekly newspaper of the International Reading Association, also announced BCL as the Library of Congress's reading promotion theme for 1993. The December 1992 - January 1993 issue followed up with a longer article, listing ideas on how to celebrate the theme drawn from the Center for the Book's BCL brochure and pointing out that the theme would remain valid through 1994.

The Library of Congress's biweekly *Information Bulletin* of December 14, 1992, announced—in its "News from the Center for the Book" section—that BCL was to be the reading promotion theme for 1993-1994.

The January 1993 issue of *Adult Literacy: Programs, Planning, Issues*, the newsletter of the Business Council for Effective Literacy, carried—under a generously proportioned reproduction of the "Books Give Us Wings" logo—an announcement of BCL as the theme of the Library of Congress's 1993-1994 reading campaign.

The January 1993 issue of *CEA News & Notes*, quarterly newsletter of the Correctional Education Association, published a front-page article announcing the CEA's co-sponsorship, with the Center for the Book, of an essay contest for inmates enrolled in a G.E.D. program, on the "Books Change Lives" theme.

The January 1993 issue of *The Written Word*, a monthly newsletter "promoting communications in the field of functional literacy," published by CEGA Services of Lincoln, Nebraska, featured Thomas Jefferson's assertion, "I cannot live without books" on its cover, and devoted its lead article (entitled "Books Change Lives") to announcing BCL as the Library of Congress's reading promotion theme for 1993-1994. The article included a partial list of suggested promotional activities drawn from the campaign brochure.

The January-February 1993 issue of *Missouri Libraries*, bimonthly publication of the Missouri State Library, informed its readers that BCL would be the Library of Congress's reading promotion theme for 1993-1994.

The spring 1993 issue of *Lutheran Libraries*, journal of the Lutheran Church Library Association, told its readers about the Library of Congress's choice of BCL as the reading promotion theme for 1993-1994 and informed them how to contact the Center for the Book for additional information.

The first page of the spring 1993 issue of *The Young Reader*, a quarterly newsletter "about children and reading" published by *The Boston Globe*, carried an announcement of the publication's celebration of BCL. It stated that the newsletter had "asked parents, librarians, teachers and book critics to select children's books that they felt might change a life. Books," it explained, "were chosen because they may lead readers to be more observant of the world around them; to realize that life is full of changes and choices, and it often takes courage to face these; to set goals and stretch to attain them; and to enjoy humor—it's a necessary spice of life." The article then listed and described 16 books, divided into "Picture Book," "Young Readers," and "Middle Readers" categories and carried comments on the theme from three authors and one author/illustrator of children's books. The newsletter also provided a form for readers to describe how a particular book changed his or her life, the writer's present age, and the age at which he or she read the book. The last page reproduced comments by children's book authors and illustrators on "How Books Change Lives."

The March 1993 issue of the American Library Association bimonthly magazine, *Book Links*, published a reproduction of the ALA's BCL poster on its cover and featured a "Books Change Lives" annotated list of 30 recommended books for young people. The books were selected by the *Book Links* Advisory Board, to "stretch the mind and stimulate the imagination...lead readers to think more deeply about the world around them, to appreciate the courage with which some people live their lives, to see beneath stereotypes, to focus on the difficult but sometimes necessary choices that people need to make, to meet outstanding role models...or to marvel at the patterns and structure of the natural world; books that have the potential to change lives." (See Appendix II).

The March 1993 issue of *Inside the Academy*, the newsletter of the Wisconsin Academy of Arts, Science, & Literature, informed its readers that BCL was the national reading theme for 1993-1994.

The *U.S. Congress Handbook*, a brochure issued by the Association of American Publishers in connection with its 23rd annual meeting, held March 24-26, 1993, in Washington, D.C., carried, on the front and back covers, an illustration of an open book, with "Books Change Lives" printed on one of its pages.

Access, bimonthly newsletter for the Library of Michigan, for March-April 1993 carried a report, with photographs, of the selection of BCL as the theme for National Book Week in February, and of "Libraries Change Lives" as that for National Library Week, both for April 1993 and April 1994. The November-December issue reproduced a photograph of the members of the board of directors of the Michigan Center for the Book, wearing T-shirts of the Center's design displaying the BCL theme.

MetroBriefs, the monthly newsletter of Metronet (an organization that covers communication, collaboration, books, reading, and literacy in the Minneapolis and Saint Paul library community), for March and April 1993, mentioned the keynote address on the subject "Books Change Lives" by Minnesota Supreme Court Associate Justice Rosalie Wahl, to be given at the fifth annual presentation, on April 23.

The American Library Association's *PR Activity Report* for April 1993 reproduced the ALA's striking BCL poster as heading to an article announcing BCL as the theme of the Library of Congress's literacy and reading promotion campaign for 1993-1994. The article mentioned the availability from ALA Graphics of BCL bookmarks, sweatshirts and T-shirts, as well as posters.

Baker & Taylor's monthly *Book Alert* for April 1993 prominently displayed the "Books Give Us Wings" logo in a version carrying both "Books Change Lives" and "The Center for the Book," at the head of an article, "After All These Years," on how—after years of neglect—"Good writing and first-rate books ...resurface and recapture attention."

The Baker & Taylor catalog, *Books For Growing Minds*, for April/May 1993, reproduced the ALA's BCL poster on cover, with the endorsement, "Baker & Taylor supports the National Reading Theme: `Books Change Lives'."

In July 1993, the International Reading Association sent a memorandum to board members, state council presidents, publications committee members, *Reading Research Quarterly* editors, *Reading Teacher* editors, affiliated editors, and professional development associates, giving them the address of the Center for the Book for obtaining information on BCL and *Developing Lifetime Readers* (the Center's review of the Library of Congress's 1991 campaign to promote literacy and reading, "The Year of the Lifetime Reader").

On August 20, 1993, the *U.S. Postal Service* issued a "Postal News" news release about the impending issuance, on October 23, of stamps honoring four classic books, mentioning that the stamps would also "be featured on a poster which salutes the theme `Books Change Lives', the 1993 national reading promotion campaign of the Library of Congress, in which the Postal Service is a partner."

The September 1993 issue of *NIE Information Service*, a "monthly subscriber publication" serving some 425 newspaper education services specialists, carried an article on Thomson Newspapers Corporation partnership with the Library of Congress. It was illustrated by one of the six advertisements designed by Thomson Newspapers Corporation to build support for local libraries, which offer newspapers as well as books to be read by the members of the public that take advantage of them.

On September 8, 1993, International Literacy Day, many of the 240 newspapers owned by the Thomson Newspapers Corporation in the United States and Canada published interviews with Librarian of Congress James H. Billington and Director of the Center for the Book John Y. Cole, thus providing Dr. Cole an opportunity to discuss the significance of the BCL theme for 1993-1994. In many of the papers the interviews appeared in "Read All About It," the Newspaper-In-Education supplement prepared by the Newspaper Association of America Foundation and sent to Newspaper Association of America affiliates across the country. Many of the supplements also carried one of a series of advertisements developed by Thomson Newspapers Corporation to develop support for local libraries (see preceding item).

The November 1993 issue of *Inside the Academy*, newsletter of the Wisconsin Academy of Sciences, Arts & Letters, announced co-sponsorship by the Wisconsin Center for the Book, with the Center for the Book in the Library of Congress, of the 1993-1994 *Read* magazine "Letters About Literature" contest on the BCL theme and provided information on how to submit entries.

The *Wilson Library Bulletin* for December 1993 carried an article, "State Centers for the Book Show How 'Books Change Lives,'" by Barbara Bryant. It described the state centers and their relationship with the Center for the Book, summarizing notable activities by the state centers, and relating them to successive national campaigns initiated by the Center for the Book and culminating in 1993-1994.

The program for the 1993 annual convention of the Modern Language Association is dedicated "to the Library of Congress Center for the Book whose 1993-1994 theme is Books Change Lives."

The January/February/March 1994 issue of *V.S.L.A. News (Virginia State Library and Archives News)* carries an article entitled, "Can A Book Change Your Life? Virginia Students Say 'Yes!'" on the Virginia winner of *Read* magazine's 1993-1994 "Letters About Literature" contest, on the BCL theme, which the Virginia Center for the Book and the Center for the Book in the Library of Congress jointly co-sponsored in Virginia.

The January 15, 1994, issue of *The National Rural Letter Carrier*, biweekly publication of the National Rural Letter Carriers' Association, carried an information item on the BCL campaign under a reproduction of the block of four U.S. postage stamps depicting classic children's books, with the explanation that the Library of Congress was a partner with the NRLCA Auxiliary's "Americanism project on Literacy."

The February 1994 issue of *NJEA Review*, official publication of the New Jersey Education Association, carried as a leading feature an article entitled, "Reading & books change lives." Illustrated with photographs of a child reading aloud, children reading together, and a mother reading with her child, it reported on the New Jersey Connection's partnership with the Center for the Book in promoting the BCL national reading theme, with extensive quotations from the BCL campaign brochure.

On February 28, 1994, the *Wall Street Journal* carried an article by staff reporter Clare Ansberry, entitled, "Dear Author: Your Book Has Changed My Life," describing the BCL "Letters About Literature" essay contest jointly sponsored by Read magazine and the Center for the Book.

The *Irving News*, a daily published in the Dallas, Texas, suburb of Irving, reported on April 21, 1994 that, at a banquet to be held at the Energy Club in Dallas, on April 26, the North Texas Association of Phi Beta Kappa would announce the winners of its essay contest for juniors in high schools in the Irving independent school district, on the BCL theme, as sponsored by the Center for the Book in the Library of Congress.

The *Publishers Weekly* of June 6 carried a half-page notice from Doubleday with the text, "**Jacqueline Kennedy Onassis 1929-1994:** Books change lives; she changed ours."

The International Reading Association bimonthly *Reading Today* for June/July 1994 devoted a two-page spread to "Books Change Lives" developments. Major items were responses from readers to the paper's appeal for brief statements on how a book has changed a reader's life; an article, illustrated with a picture of essay contest winner Aslum Khan receiving an "I Cannot Live Without Books" T-shirt from Center for the Book director John Y. Cole, on the Weekly Reader Corporation's *Read* magazine BCL essay contest; and a reprint of Rickey Smith's essay, "The Effect of *The Autobiography of Malcolm X*" (see page 27), which won the 1993 Correctional Education Association's BCL essay contest.

The July 15, 1994, issue of *Leadership News*, newsletter of the American Association of School Administrators, carried an announcement and thumbnail description of the BCL campaign and provided the address of the Center for the Book for those readers interested in obtaining more information.

MetroBriefs, the newsletter for the Minneapolis-Saint Paul Metronet organization, reported in July 1994 that the Minnesota Center for the Book would once again be a state sponsor for *Read* magazine's "Letters for Literature" contest on the theme, "Books Change Lives."

The July-August 1994 issue of *Missouri Libraries*, a publication of the Missouri State Library, featured an announcement of the Missouri Center for the Book's participation as a co-sponsor of the Weekly Reader Corporation's *Read* magazine's 1994-1995 "Letters About Literature" contest on the BCL theme, with the Weekly Reader Corporation and the Center for the Book in the Library of Congress.

The July-August 1994 issue of *The Library of Virginia*, newsletter of the Virginia State Library and Archives, publicized *Books Change Lives: Quotes to Treasure*, a new ALA publication celebrating the BCL theme.

A cover article in the August 1994 issue of the newsletter of the Phi Beta Kappa North Texas Association, *Keynotes*, reported on the association's awarding of prizes on April 26 to "its first *Books Change Lives* contest winners," expressing the association's hope "to expand the *Books Change Lives* competition to other school districts in the North Texas area through contributions from Phi Beta Kappa members and the community at large."

The fall 1994 issue of *Preface: Preview of Literary Events*, quarterly newsletter of the Florida Center for the Book announced *Read* magazine's forthcoming 1994-1995 "Letters About Literature" contest using the BCL theme, once again co-sponsored in the state by the Florida Center for the Book.

The September 5, 1994, issue of the Library of Congress's biweekly *Information Bulletin* devoted almost a full page to a summary report on BCL campaign developments in various parts of the country.

The September-October 1994 issue of the Virginia State Library's newsletter, *The Library of Virginia* (previously, V.S.L.A. News) reported the involvement of the Virginia Center for the Book as a co-sponsor of the 1994-1995 *Read* magazine "Letters About Literature" contest, which has BCL as its theme.

During 1994, the *Highsmith Co., Inc.*, of Fort Atkinson, Wisconsin, a catalog marketing operation selling library equipment and library promotional items, offered a beverage mugs, bookmarks, buttons, plastic bags, and T-shirts for sale, all promoting the BCL theme.

The Graphics Division of the American Library Association commissioned and printed a BCL poster which received wide national distribution both directly from the ALA and, in a version that carried the Center's name, from the Center for the Book, which alone distributed several thousand copies to the state centers for the book and the Reading Promotion Partners (see front cover).

The spring-summer 1993 issue of *A Reader's Catalogue*, a mail-order catalog issued by Cahill & Company, of St. Paul, Minnesota, carried Thomas Jefferson's assertion, "I cannot live without books" on the back cover.

In mid-1993, the International Book Bank issued a handsome poster guide, celebrating BCL on one side, while the reverse side contained information on the IBB's 1992 book shipments, and its relationships with such organizations as the Center for the Book in the Library of Congress, the U.S. Information Agency, and the National Association of College Stores.

In September 1993, the New Jersey Connection brought out the 1993 edition of its annual *A Book of New Jersey Students' Writings About Reading*, its cover embellished with the Connection's version of the national reading promotion theme, "Books Change Lives—READ!" and also carrying the "Books Give Us Wings" slogan included in the Center for the Book logo. Printed by Jersey City Power & Light and distributed by United Jersey Bank "to every school media center and public library in New Jersey" and carrying an introductory letter from New Jersey First Lady Mrs. Lucinda Florio, the book contains prose statements and poems by readers, from first grade to 18-year-olds, on books that had changed their lives. The Connection's success in building community support was evident from the "Corporate Partners in Reading" listed in the front of the book, which included a bank, a bookshop, a cable TV firm, and a supermarket chain, as well as Seton Hall University, and major national and international companies, all with a presence in New Jersey, such as CPC International, Gannet Outdoor, Lipton, Macy's, Pepsi Cola, Prudential Insurance, and the international pharmaceutical company Sandoz. The Connection also brought out a poster (widely displayed in the state), headed with "Books Change Lives—READ!" and honoring the eight 1993 winners of the New Jersey Enthusiastic Readers Award, showing them in the Drumthwacket, the governor's mansion in Princeton, standing and seated around New Jersey First Lady Lucinda Florio.

In May 1994, the American Library Association's Booklist Publications issued *Books Change Lives: Quotes to Treasure*, a collection of testimonials on the value of books and reading by 39 authors and illustrators of children's books.

In September 1994 the New Jersey Connection brought out a poster, embellished with "Reading Changes Lives—READ!" (the Connection's variation on BCL for the second year of the campaign), honoring eight recipients of the 1994 New Jersey Enthusiastic Reader award. The poster carries in the upper left-hand corner a reproduction of the open-book logo of the Center for the Book, with the slogan, "Give Us Books Give Us Wings"

Also in September, the New Jersey Connection issued the 1994 edition of *A Book of New Jersey Students Writing about Reading*. The cover carries the slogans, "Reading Changes Lives—READ!," "Books Can Change the World!," and "Books Give Us Wings." The publication includes a reproduction of the governor's proclamation of BCL as the state reading theme for 1994.

"Books Change Lives" was celebrated in different ways across the country.

Alpha Kappa Alpha Sorority, Inc. In late 1992, the Alpha Kappa Alpha Sorority distributed 850 BCL brochures to its chapters across the country.

Altrusa International Foundation. In April 1993, at the request of the Foundation chairman, the Center for the Book sent BCL brochures, logo sheets, and bookmarks to members of the Foundation's parent Altrusa International Association in 20 states and Puerto Rico, and two foreign countries, England and New Zealand.

American Association for the Advancement of Science. The August/September issue of *Science Books & Films*, a bimonthly publication of the American Association for the Advancement of Science (AAAS), carried a lead article, "Science Books Change Lives," devoted to the responses of Dr. Murray Gell-Mann (who was awarded the 1969 Nobel prize in physics for discovering the quark), other AAAS members, and reviewers for *Science Books & Films*, to an appeal from the magazine to members to describe the books that have changed their lives. Books cited reflected a remarkable diversity of taste, ranging from *The Art of Scientific Investigation*, by William B. Beveridge, *The Rise of the New Physics: Its Mathematical and Physical Theories* by A. d'Abro, *The Double Helix* by James D. Watson, and *Fleas, Flukes and Cuckoos. A Study of Bird Parasites*, on the one hand, to the *Complete Book of Marvels* by Richard Halliburton, *Alice in Wonderland* by Lewis Carroll, *Finnegan's Wake* by James Joyce, and *The Elements of Style* by William Strunk and E.B. White, on the other.

American Association of Community Colleges. The April/May 1994 issue of the *Community College Journal*, in an item announcing that the AACC had become a Reading Promotion Partner, described the "AACC and its member colleges" as "prime examples of organizations that subscribe to the. . .theme, 'Books Change Lives.'"

American Association of School Administrators. The July 15, 1994 issue of *Leadership News*, the semi-monthly newsletter of the AASA, carried an item, "Literacy Campaign Promotes Books," on the BCL campaign and the AASA's involvement in it as a Reading Promotion Partner of the Library. It refers readers to the Center for additional information.

American Library Association. The American Library Association monthly, *American Libraries*, for April 1993, drawing on a popular variation of the BCL theme, carried an article, entitled "Actors, writers, sports stars agree: Libraries do change lives," subtitled, "Libraries make a difference in the lives of their users; testimonials may make a difference in the lives of libraries." Among those whose supportive statements appeared in the article were Ray Bradbury, novelist; Vincent E. "Bo" Jackson, baseball player; James A. Michener, novelist; Gloria Estefan, singer, Janet Leigh, actress; Dave Barry, newspaper columnist; John H. Johnson, CEO of Johnson Publishing Company, publisher of *Ebony*; and Hugh Downs, television newscaster. That same month, the ALA's PR *Activity Report* also reported prominently on the BCL campaign: see Publicity, above. The Association selected a variation on BCL, "Libraries Change Lives," to be the theme of National Library Week (April 17-23) in 1994.

American Mensa, Ltd. In January 1994, American Mensa, Ltd., decided that their 1994 project, designated Project Inkslinger, would be to re-stock public libraries devastated by floods: one, the Donaphin County public library in Elwood, Kansas, another the Grand Canyon Library in Arizona. Each book supplied by American Mensa would carry a bookplate showing the Center for the Book logo, the theme "Books Change Lives" and the explanatory text, "Contributed by your friends in Mensa, A Flood of Books 1994." In March, Project Inkslinger expanded to re-stock a library in New York state also devastated by floods. As it developed the project received attention from the press in widely separated parts of the country—New Hampshire, Oklahoma, South Carolina, and Texas.

Association of American Publishers. The association decorated the front and back covers of the *U.S. Congress Handbook* with an illustration of an open book and the phrase, "Books Change Lives." The brochure was issued in connection with the association's 23rd annual meeting, held in Washington, D.C., March 24-26, 1993.

Association of Junior Leagues International. In the summer of 1994, the Association of Junior Leagues International distributed BCL brochures to all 287 Junior Leagues in the United States, Canada, Mexico, and the United Kingdom.

Auxiliary of the National Rural Letter Carriers' Association. In January 1994, the National Rural Letter Carriers' Association's biweekly publication, *The National Rural Letter Carrier*, carried a news item on the partnership between the Auxiliary and the Library of Congress in promoting literacy (see "Publicity" above). In April, the Auxiliary received delivery of 1,500 BCL brochures and, in June, of 25 U.S. Postal Service "Curl Up With a Good Stamp" posters, for distribution to its members.

Cartoonists Across America (CAA). In July 1994, CAA issued a press release announcing that on September 8 (International Literacy Day) artists would finish painting the "world's largest literacy mural" on a 53-foot trailer truck, parked at the Library of Congress for the day, adding to the composition the Center for the Book's slogan, "Books Change Lives," to celebrate the 1994 theme. The trailer truck—its sides decorated with painted literacy cartoons and slogans, including the newly added BCL—was parked all day in front of the James Madison Memorial Building of the Library of Congress, on Independence Avenue, S.E., in Washington, D.C. The artistic efforts of CAA members were supplemented by those of Head Start children and passers-by, who (temporarily equipped by the CAA members with brushes and pots of paint) freshened the older, more weatherbeaten painting, while trained artists worked on adding new images to the composition.

Chautauqua Institution. The Chautauqua Literary and Scientific Circle class of 1993, influenced by the dramatic changes that had occurred in the world since the class's formation in 1989 (the dissolution of the Soviet Union, the Iraqi occupation of Kuwait, the Gulf War, the release from prison of Nelson Mandela, among others, and the Institution's partnership with the Library of Congress) chose a variation on the BCL theme as its class motto: "Reading Changes the World Family."

Correctional Education Association. The Correctional Education Association announced in January 1993 its sponsorship, in partnership with the Center for the Book, of an essay contest for students currently enrolled in a GED program. The essay "should describe how a book, fiction or nonfiction, changed the student's life and should discuss how specific ideas, events or characters in the book suggested that change."

The October issue of CEA News & Notes, the association's quarterly newsletter, carried as its lead article the winning essay in this contest, entitled "The Effect of The Autobiography of Malcolm X," by Rickey Smith, of the Sumter Correctional Institution in Florida (see page 27). A front-page sidebar mentions that Ann Robinson of Rappahannock Security Center in Virginia received an honorable mention, for her pre-GED essay on *Charlotte's Web*.

In March 1994, the Correctional Education Association announced its third annual essay contest, conducted in partnership with the Center for the Book in the Library of Congress, for inmates enrolled in GED courses. As in 1993, the "Books Change Lives" theme was used, with the winning essay to be printed in the CEA's quarterly newsletter, and a 57-book collection donated by the New Readers Press, a subsidiary of Laubach Literacy Action, to go to the winning contestant's teacher to serve as a classroom library. The Center for the Book supplied three of its BCL T-shirts, with "I Cannot Live Without Books" emblazoned on the front, to go to those who placed 1st, 2nd, and 3rd place in the contest.

In October 1994, the Center for the Book responded to an appeal for help from the library of the Gowanda Correctional Facility (Gowanda, New York) presumably stimulated by publicity about the BCL campaign by the CEA, by sending it 200 BCL brochures, a BCL poster, a U.S. Postal Service "Curl Up With a Good Stamp" poster, and other campaign-related material.

CEA News and Notes for October/November 1994 carried as its lead article the winning essay of its 1994 BCL essay contest, "How Maya Angelou's Childhood and Hardships Affected My life," by Jimmie Willoughby (see page 31), a commentary on Angelou's *I Know Why the Caged Bird Sings*. A note on the front page commented on the "many excellent entries this year," the "increased numbers of participants"..."due in part to the efforts of the Federal Bureau of Prisons whose teachers and administrators encouraged their students to enter, and to the generosity of the New Readers Press," which "donated a library of 57 books to the classroom of the teacher whose student submitted the winning essay."

Distance Education and Training Council. In late 1992 the Distance Education and Training Council distributed 100 BCL brochures to the correspondence schools accredited by the Council.

Federal Bureau of Prisons (U.S. Department of Justice). On May 5, 1994, the Federal Bureau of Prisons informed its Regional Education Administrators of its decision to participate in the Correctional Education Association's third annual essay contest for inmates in GED courses, with contributions to be written on the theme BCL.

First Book. In the late spring of 1994, First Book, in partnership with the **Association of Junior Leagues International** and the **Corporation for Public Broadcasting**, and supported by the CFB, began working on a program for acquiring books for children who had none. A pilot project, linked with the **Corporation for Public Broadcasting's** "Ready For School" program, began at three public television stations (WETA in Washington; WGBH in Boston; and WGTE in Toledo) in October. Bookplates in each of the books carried the logos of the four partners, and the Center for the Book logo a variation carrying the BCL theme.

General Federation of Women's Clubs International. On June 18-22, 1994, at its annual convention held in Atlanta, Georgia, the GFWC International distributed 275 BCL brochures along with other Center for the Book materials. Between July 1 and October 20, the following state federations and individual member clubs requested and received, for distribution to their members, a some 1,300 BCL brochures, 14 BCL posters, 16 BCL bookmarks, and other informational and promotional material: the Arizona, Arkansas, Florida, Maryland, Mississippi, New Hampshire, Tennessee, Texas, Virginia, and West Virginia Federations; the Carrizozo (Arizona) Women's Club, the Cartersville (Georgia) Women's Club, the Chicago Heights (Illinois) Junior Women's Club, the Coal City (Illinois) Junior Women's Club, and the Lexington (North Carolina) Women's Club. On September 10, in response to an invitation to address a meeting of the GFWC International's board of directors on the mission and activities of the Center for the Book and their relationship to the literacy programs of the GFWC, Michael Thompson, a consultant to the Center, gave board members an overview of the composition of the Reading Promotion Partners of the Library of Congress and described their activities, with special emphasis on the role of the partners in the BCL campaign.

International Book Bank (IBB). The IBB's annual report for 1992, issued in the form of an attractive poster guide, asserted that its new partnership with the Library of Congress was "grounded in the shared belief that 'Books Change Lives.'"

International Reading Association (IRA). The October-November 1992 issue of *Reading Today*, bimonthly newspaper of the IRA, under the heading "Books Change Lives," stated, "Each of us has read a book at some point that has had a special influence on us—that has indeed changed our lives. In recognition of this fact, the Center for the Book in the U.S. Library of Congress has selected "Books Change Lives" as its reading promotion theme for 1993. We encourage IRA councils and members to incorporate this theme into their activities during 1993." After reminding readers that BCL was the Library of Congress reasing promotion theme for 1993-94, the newspaper listed ideas drawn from the campaign brochure that organizations might use to celebrate the theme.

The April-May 1993 issue of *Reading Today* devoted a half page, headed "Books Change Lives," to three items related to the BCL campaign. One was a report on the January 28 partners "idea-exchange" meeting at the Library of Congress. Another was an article entitled, "Books Change Lives: One Example," describing the transforming effect of reading on a non-reader who had casually bought three books from a second-hand bookshop when bored: four years later he owned a library of over 200 books! And the third was an invitation to readers (1) to submit brief articles (250 words or fewer) that describe how books have changed their lives, and (2) to send in a list containing the title and author of the one children's book, one adult book, and one professional education book that have had the greatest influence in their lives; *Reading Today* would compile these titles for a future article. The invitation was repeated in the June-July issue and the December 1993 -January 1994 issue carried the first responses. The June-July 1994 printed additional ones.

In July 1994, the IRA—looking ahead to the celebration of International Literacy Day on September 8, prepared a list of "Suggestions for International Literacy Day Activities" for distribution to persons asking the IRA for information on International Literacy Day. The suggestions were based on the "Ideas for Changing Lives" section of the Center for the Book's BCL brochure.

In October, the IRA included a BCL brochure in a "partnership packet" of information from a "range of organizations with shared interests in literacy" that it sent to approximately 1,300 reading council officers of the Association.

The December 1994/January 1995 issue of *Reading Today* carried a third and final article reproducing responses from readers to the paper's appeal to submit a brief statement on the book that had most influenced the reader's life.

Laubach Literacy Action (LLA). At its biennial convention held in Little Rock, Arkansas (June 2-5, 1994) LLA distributed 500 BCL brochures along with other CFB materials. LLA's affiliated New Reader's Press, which publishes books designed to appeal to adult new readers, donated a complete series of 57 titles to the Correctional Education Association, to be awarded to the teacher of the winning contestant in the CEA's 1994 BCL essay contest for inmates enrolled in GED classes, cosponsored for the first time by the Federal Bureau of Prisons.

The Links, Inc. At its biennial convention, held in Louisville, Kentucky, from June 27 to July 2, 1994, The Links, Inc. distributed 250 BCL posters in the framework of its National Services to Youth program.

Lutheran Church Library Association (LCLA). The fall 1992 issue of *LCLA Chapter Open Mike*, quarterly newsletter of the Lutheran Church Library Association, made the first public announcement of BCL as the Library of Congress's reading promotion theme for 1993-1994 and gave a summary description of the Center for the Book's mission and the Center's role in earlier campaigns, concluding, "LCLA is pleased to be among 110 other organizations who have joined together as "Partners of the Library of Congress" in the promotion of their yearly reading promotion campaigns." The article then cited the American Library Association, the American Booksellers Association, the Barbara Bush Foundation for Family Literacy, the Children's Book Council, Inc., the Christian Booksellers' Association, Laubach Literacy Action, the National Center for Family Literacy, and Reading Is Fundamental as examples of "these fine organizations." The spring and fall 1993 issues carried a further announcement of the campaign and supplied the address of the Center for the Book for use by any association member who wished to obtain additional information. The spring 1994 issue appealed to its readers to submit to the LCLA office at their ear-

liest convenience, promotional items, pictures, newsletter items illustrating innovative ways they have used the theme to advance their own literacy and/or reading promotion projects. The items, the article explained, were then to be forwarded to the Center for the Book for inclusion in the projected review of the campaign. Under a different heading, the same issue provided a summary account of the mission of the Center, describing the involvement of Reading Promotion Partners in the campaign, mentioning again the planned review and describing the Center's involvement in the design of the U.S. Postal Service poster featuring four 29-cent stamps honoring classic children's books. The fall 1994 issue drew the attention of its readers to the American Library Association booklet, *Books Change Lives: Quotes to Treasure*.

Modern Language Association of America. The November 1993 issue of *PMLA*, bimonthly of the Modern Language Association of America, dedicated the program of the Association's annual convention "to the Library of Congress Center for the Book, whose 1993-1994 theme is Books Change Lives."

National Alliance of Black School Educators. *NewsBriefs*, the quarterly newsletter of the National Alliance of Black School Educators that came out in May 1993, carried on its front cover a reproduction of the BCL version of the Center for the Book logo.

National Association for the Education of Young Children. In March 1993, the Abilene, Texas, affiliate of the National Association for the Education of Young Children requested and received 300 BCL brochures for local distribution.

National Association of Colored Women's Clubs. The Association distributed 500 BCL brochures at its biennial national convention, held in Oklahoma City, in July 1994.

National Catholic Education Association. The NCEA monthly newsletter, *NCEA Notes*, for November 1992 carried an item announcing BCL as a "unifying theme for organizing and supporting literacy projects that benefit all age groups." The November 1993 issue used the CFB's "Books Change Lives" poster to decorate an exhortation to "Remember National Young Reader's Day, November 17, 1993."

National Conference of Lieutenant Governors. The spring 1993 issue of *NCLG Focus*, the quarterly newsletter of the National Conference of Lieutenant Governors, used nearly half a page for a prominent announcement, illustrated with the "Books Give Us Wings" logo, of BCL as the Library of Congress reading promotion theme for 1993-1994. The announcement quoted extensively from the campaign brochure and asked Conference members to inform the NCLG secretariat of any programs initiated following suggestions in the brochure. In a follow-up, Michael Thompson, a consultant to the Center for the Book, spoke on invitation at a lunch meeting of the NCLG, held in Washington on March 24, 1994. After stressing the importance of literate and reading general public for the health of a representative democracy, he provided information on the Center for the Book and its programs, with special emphasis on the BCL campaign and the role in it of Reading Promotion Partners and the state centers for the book.

National Council of Negro Women. In connection with the display of the Center for the Book's BCL posters at all seven of the NCNW's Black Family Reunion Celebrations (held in Atlanta, Chicago, Cincinnati, Los Angeles, Memphis, Philadelphia, and Washington, D.C. during the months of July through September, 1993 and 1994), the NCNW offered participants its Black Family Reading Pledge Cards, along with copies of a brochure on "African American Literature for Young Children" developed by the National Black Child Development Institute. The pledge form, headed "The NCNW Black Family Reading Pledge," announced the NCNW's involvement with the Center for the Book's promotion of interest in reading, books, and learning through the print media and, after quoting the statement of founder Mary McLeod Bethune, "The whole world opened to me when I learned to read," carried the exhortation, "Remember—Books Change Lives!"

National Federation of Press Women. Capital Press Women, an affiliate of the National Federation of Press Women, incorporated a variation of the BCL theme, "Take the Lead/Learn to Read/Newspapers Change Lives" in flyers distributed by the Literacy Volunteers of America and included in public service announcements on local radio stations in preparation for a March 1993 National Capital area Family Literacy Event co-sponsored with the Literacy Volunteers of America and the Washington Times.

National Newspaper Foundation. On March 10, 1994, the National Newspaper Association, which represents the interests of more than 4,600 community newspapers across the country and for which the National Newspaper Foundation is a non-profit affiliate, co-sponsored with the Center for the Book a lunch in the Montpelier Room for its members attending the NNA's 33rd Annual Congressional Affairs Conference. The Librarian of Congress and the Director of the Center for the Book both addressed the lunch, which was also attended by more than 20 members of Congress.

New Jersey Connection. In the fall of 1992, the New Jersey Connection mailed to its approximately 4,000 members, including all New Jersey schools and libraries, a ten-page booklet listing its suggestions for promoting the BCL theme and the awards it would be making in 1993. The booklet cover carried the heading, "1993 - Books Change Lives!," followed by the exhortation: "Celebrate the Joys of Reading." Inside, on pages adorned with a reproduction of the Center's "Books Change Lives" slogan, a letter by the Executive Director announces the BCL theme for 1993 and 1994 and lists projected New Jersey Connection activities for the period: readathons; the annual "New Jersey Enthusiastic Reader Awards" to a student in each of the primary and secondary school grades in each of the three zones into which the Connection has divided the state; the Connection's annual *Young People's Book*, a book of writing about reading by students in New Jersey schools; and the "New Jersey Enthusiastic Librarian or Teacher Award," a new annual award for "teachers or librarians who exhibits enthusiasm in their reading programs." The remainder of the mailing consisted of entry and nomination forms for the awards and the *Young People's Book*.

In the fall of 1993, the New Jersey Connection once again mailed out its booklet, giving suggestions for promoting the theme for 1994 (this time, the variation, "Reading Changes Lives") and listing the awards it would make during the coming year. The booklet cover was decorated with the assertion, "1994 - Reading Changes Lives: Celebrate the Joys of READING," above a drawing of a girl reading a book entitled *Metamorphosis* which rests on a table emblazoned, "Reading Changes Lives, See the Difference." The New Jersey Connection also issued a 1993 "New Jersey Enthusiastic Readers Award" poster, showing—under the headline "Books Change Lives—READ!"—the seven winners of the award with New Jersey First Lady Lucinda Florio. The poster prominently displayed a version of the Center for the Book logo, with the slogan "Give Us Books, Give Us Wings." The *Book of New Jersey Students' Writing About Reading* issued in the fall of 1993 carried on its cover both "Books Change Lives—READ!" and "Books Give Us Wings."

Newspaper Association of America Foundation (NAA). In a follow-up in July 1994 to discussions held with a Center for the Book representative at the NAA Foundation's annual Newspaper-in-Education (NIE) meeting, May 25-27 in Memphis, Tennessee, the NIE coordinator for *Kingsport Times-News* requested and received from the center 150 BCL brochures for distribution at a local teacher workshop.

Phi Beta Kappa Society. The spring 1993 issues of the society's quarterly newsletter, *The Key Reporter*, under the heading, "Phi Beta Kappa Supports 'Books Change Lives' Project," invited chapters and alumni associations "to use the theme for existing or new projects celebrating literacy and reading." The June issue carried a second announcement of the campaign. In response, the Center for the Book received almost 50 letters requesting campaign material from chapters, alumni associations, and individual members of the Society. On December 9, the Secretary-Treasurer of the North Texas Association of Phi Beta Kappa, writing from Dallas, informed the Center for the Book of a "Books Change Lives" pilot project in the Dallas-Fort Worth metroplex area: an essay contest entitled "Books Change Lives - a Call for Papers," open to all high school juniors in the Irving Independent School District. Contestants should submit essays on how a literary work had affected their life, with a $1,000 scholarship prize going to the winner and a $500 gift to the library in the winner's school, all entries to be received by March 1, 1994. The association also distributed BCL brochures to Irving Independent School District Administrators, on a district level and on a high school level. In January 1994, the association issued the first number of a newsletter, the *Phi Beta Kappa North Texas Association News*, with the lead article, "Books Change Lives' Scholarship Competition," devoted to a description of its pilot project, "inspired by the 1993-1994 reading promotional theme of the Library of Congress." It also used a BCL stamp on envelopes in official correspondence.

On April 26, at its 45th annual meeting, the North Texas Association awarded 1st, 2nd and 3rd prizes for submissions in its BCL essay contest for juniors attending high school in the Irving, Texas, independent school district. The first prize (a $1,000 scholarship and a gift of $500 worth of books to his school's library) went to Scott Hocutt of Irving High School for "The Ruminations of a Philosopher Emperor," an essay on the Meditations of Marcus Aurelius (see page 16). Speakers at the dinner were Lee Cullom, columnist for the *Dallas Morning News*, who spoke on "American Culture: Can It Be both Moral and Free," and Michael Thompson, consultant to the Center for the Book, who spoke on "The Center for the Book and Phi Beta Kappa, a Working Partnership."

On October 30, the president of the association informed the Center for the Book of its success in raising funds from Texas Instruments and Brinker International, which along with other monies, would enable it to launch a second "Books Change Lives" essay competition later in the year, in two additional north Texas school districts, as well as in the Irving district, the site of the competition announced in 1993.

The winter 1994-1995 issue of *The Key Reporter*, in a summary article, "Alumni Associations: 1993-1994 Donations, Activities," reported the results of the North Texas Association's first "Books Change Lives" essay contest.

Phi Beta Sigma Fraternity, Inc. The Phi Beta Sigma Fraternity distributed BCL campaign materials to its seven Regional Directors and its Metropolitan Area chapters, for use during regional, state, and area meetings.

SER - Jobs for Progress, Inc. The SER/IBM Business Institute of Miami, Florida, a division of SER - Jobs for Progress, received three of the Center's BCL posters in August 1993, in response to a request for posters "to motivate our students to achieve their reading goals."

Southern Newspaper Publishers Association. The Southern Newspaper Publishers Association advised its member newspapers in 14 states (Alabama, Arkansas, Florida, Georgia, Kentucky, Mississippi, North Carolina, Oklahoma, South Carolina, Tennessee, Texas, Virginia, and West Virginia) to use the variation, "Newspapers Change Lives."

Thomson Newspapers Corporation. During the fall of 1993, the Director of Literacy Education for the Thomson Newspapers Corporation arranged for representatives from the Indiana, Ohio, and Wisconsin centers for the book and from the Center for the Book in the Library of Congress to speak on the BCL campaign and partnership with the Library to cluster meetings of the group's NIE coordinators. In September, each of the roughly 240 Thomson-owned newspapers in the United States and Canada received a set of six camera-ready advertisements that related the promotion of literacy and reading to the BCL campaign and to Thomson Newspapers' support for local libraries. Each advertisement carried, near the top, the sentence, "Newspapers and books change lives" and, near the bottom, "Support your local library," and, in the lower right-hand corner the "Books Give Us Wings" logo, ascribed to "The Center for the Book, Library of Congress." The advertisements began appearing in Thomson-owned newspapers that same month. Also in September, as additional support for its NIE program, the Thomson Newspapers Corporation started distributing to member newspapers brochures headed "Newspapers Change Lives," some subtitled "Family Library Fun" and others, "School Library Fun,"—all of them urging their readers to "Make newspaper reading a part of your trip to the library and a part of your daily routine!" and offering suggestions of ways to benefit at home and in school from regularly reading newspapers. In October the Corporation's Director of Literacy Education distributed to Newspaper-in-Education coordinators of its member newspapers 200 copies of the first issue of *Partner's Update*, a newsletter for Reading Promotion Partners of the Library of Congress issued by the Center for the Book (see also National Events, on page 45).

U.S. Department of Defense Dependents' Schools. On January 10, 1994, the Director of the Department of Defense Dependents' Schools, Pacific Region, issued his 7th annual Director's Challenge in Reading, addressed to students and, at the discretion of the principal, to members of the DoD community in the region. Participants were challenged to read an assigned amount of reading (the amount to be set by each principal). Those completing the assigned amount would receive a certificate from the director. Each school/community was also challenged to reach a combined goal in reading, that goal either to involve having a set percentage of participants completing the Challenge, reading a pre-set total of pages, books, or completing an assigned number of minutes/hours of reading, the goal to be set by the school. The Director would award a plaque to schools/communities reaching their combined goals. Reading by one person to another would count; reading textbooks would not. The emphasis would be on reading outside of school, but reading of appropriate material in school would count, too.

U.S. Department of Education. The October 1992 issue of *A.L.L. Points Bulletin*, bimonthly newsletter of the Adult Education and Literacy Division of the U.S. Department of Education, under a reproduction of the BCL logo and the words, "Center for the Book: An Active Partner in Promoting Literacy," announced BCL as the theme of the Library of Congress's 1993-94 campaign, in the course of an article describing the Center's role in stimulating public interest in books and reading. The February 1994 issue of the *Bulletin*, once again illustrated with the BCL version of the Center's logo, reported to its readers that the campaign had "so far been joined by nearly 30 affiliated state centers for the book and 128 reading promotion partners that reflect a spectacular diversity of constituencies."

U.S. Department of Health and Human Services. *Children Today*, occasional publication of the Administration for Children and Families of the Department of Health and Human Services, carried an item in its final issue for 1994 describing the participation of children enrolled in the Head Start program in the BCL event, co-sponsored by the Center for the Book and Cartoonists Across America celebrating International Literacy Day, September 8, 1994.

U.S. Postal Service. The Center for the Book distributed approximately 10,000 of the U.S. Postal Service's popular "Curl Up With a Good Stamp" posters, honoring four childhood classics and carrying the CFB logo with "Books Change Lives." The bulk went to schools and libraries that had written in to the Center, to the state centers, and to the Reading Promotion Partners. Among the partners, the heaviest users were the American Association of School Administrators, the Association of Booksellers to Children, the Bureau of Federal Prisons, and the Girl Scouts of the U.S.A., the National Association of Secondary School Principals.

Weekly Reader Corporation. On October 29, 1993, *Read* magazine, owned by the Weekly Reader Corporation, announced a new annual BCL writing contest, co-sponsored with the Center for the Book. Each contestant was to write a letter of 1000 words or fewer to the author of his or her favorite book, explaining what the book taught the contestant about him/herself, and send it to "Books Change Lives," at the Corporation's head office, at 245 Long Hill Road, P.O. Box 2791, Middletown, CT 06457-9251. The grand-prize winner would win an all-expenses-paid trip to the Library of Congress, in the company of a parent or a guardian over the age of 21, to be the guest of honor at a luncheon at the Center for the Book, and on the three subsequent days have the chance to tour the White House, the Air and Space Museum, the war memorials, and much more. In addition *Read* and participating state centers for the book would award a number of finalist prizes, each finalist to receive a cash award of $100. Ten state centers—those in Connecticut, Florida, Iowa, Illinois, Michigan, Minnesota, North Dakota, Ohio, Virginia, and Wisconsin—participated in the 1993-1994. Participants in 1994-1995 were: Colorado, Florida, Illinois, Michigan, Minnesota, Missouri, North Dakota, Ohio, Oregon, Texas, Virginia, and Wisconsin.

Women's National Book Association. In August 1992, the Nashville chapter of the WNBA used the BCL theme on a combined informative brochure and membership application form, which set out the chapter's purpose, listed its program for 1992-1993, and described chapter activities. The winter/spring, 1992-1993, issue of the WNBA's official publication, *The Bookwoman*, announced the association's support of the BCL campaign and suggested chapters participate as a way of increasing local visibility and support, as well as further encouraging literacy and reading. In November 1993, the New York chapter organized its monthly program meeting around the BCL theme. The January/February 1994 issue of the chapter newsletter, *Did You Know?*, in an account of the November meeting's focus on the BCL theme, reported that "the sentiments of the featured speakers showed that reading is more than just an escape or an enhancement. For many people it lends substance to other aspects of living." Speakers include therapist Helen Margalith, professional writer Joan Kennedy Taylor, novelist Cathleen Schine, volunteer coordinator for the New York Book Fair to Help the Homeless Amy Mintzer, and *Fierce Attachments* author Vivian Gornick.

BOOKS CHANGE LIVES

Appendices

A LIST OF BOOKS MENTIONED IN PART ONE

The latest and/or least expensive paperback edition of each book is listed. Where no paperback exists, the hardcover edition is listed.

Adamson, Joy. *Born Free.* Pantheon, 1987.

Alcott, Louisa May. *Little Women.* Airmont Classics, 1966.

Angelou, Maya. *I Know Why the Caged Bird Sings.* Bantam, 1971.

Aurelius Antonius, Marcus. *The Meditations.* Pocket Classic Series, 1993.

Beveridge, William I. *Art of Scientific Investigation.* Vintage, 1960.

Blume, Judy. *It's Not the End of the World.* Bantam, 1979.

Burroughs, John. Deep Woods: *A John Burroughs Reader.* Peregrine Smith, 1990.

Camus, Albert. *The Plague.* Vintage, 1991.

Carroll, Lewis. *Alice's Adventures in Wonderland.* Puffin Books, 1985.

Catton, Bruce. *This Hallowed Ground.* Doubleday, 1956.

Cervantes Saavedra, Miguel de. *Don Quixote.* Viking Child Books, 1979.

Clancy, Tom. *Clear and Present Danger.* Berkley, 1990.

Clancy, Tom. *Hunt for Red October.* Berkley, 1985.

Crane, Stephen. *The Red Badge of Courage.* Airmont Classics, 1964.

D'Abro, A. *The Rise of the New Physics.* 2 volumes. Dover, 1950.

Deaver, Julie Reece. *Say Goodnight, Gracie.* HarperCollins Child's Books, 1989.

Dickens, Charles. *A Tale of Two Cities.* Bantam, 1989.

Dillard, Annie. *Pilgrim at Tinker Creek.* HarperCollins, 1988.

Doyle, Arthur Conan. *The Hound of the Baskervilles.* Airmont Classics, 1965.

Frank, Anne. *The Diary of a Young Girl.* Bantam, 1993.

Gies, Miep and Alison L. Gold. *Anne Frank Remembered: The Story of the Woman Who Helped Hide the Frank Family.* Simon & Schuster, 1988.

Gilbert, Martin. *Holocaust: History of the Jews of Europe During the Second World War.* Henry Holt, 1987.

Golding, William. *Lord of the Flies.* Berkley, 1959.

Gornick, Vivian. *Fierce Attachments.* Simon & Schuster, 1988.

Gunther, John. *Death Be Not Proud.* HarperCollins, 1989.

Haley, Alex, ed. *The Autobiography of Malcolm X.* Ballantine, 1992.

Halliburton, Richard. *Complete Book of Marvels.* (out of print)

Hawthorne, Nathaniel. *The Scarlet Letter.* Dover.

Hemingway, Ernest. *The Old Man and the Sea.* Macmillan/Collier, 1987.

Hinckley, Jack and Joann. *Breaking Point.* (out of print)

Hugo, Victor. *Les Miserables.* Translation by Norman Denny. Viking/Penguin, 1989.

Huxley, Aldous. *Brave New World.* HarperCollins, 1989.

Joyce, James. *Finnegan's Wake.* Viking/Penguin, 1982.

Lawrence, D. H. *The Rainbow.* NAL-Dutton, 1991.

Lewis, Carl and Jeffrey Marx. *Inside Track.* Simon & Schuster, 1990.

Lindwer, Willy. *The Last Seven Months of Anne Frank.* Doubleday, 1992.

Lopez, Barry. *Arctic Dreams.* Bantam, 1989.

Lowenfeld, Viktor and W. Lambert Brittain. *Creative and Mental Growth*, 8th edition. Macmillan, 1987.

Machiavelli, Niccolo. *The Prince.* Dutton, 1952.

Porter, Katharine Anne. *Ship of Fools.* Little Brown, 1984.

Rawls, Wilson. *Where the Red Fern Grows.* Bantam, 1984.

Sagan, Carl and Ann Druyan. *Shadows of Forgotten Ancestors.* Ballantine, 1993

Salinger, J. D. *The Catcher in the Rye.* Little Brown, 1991.

Sinclair, Upton. *The Jungle.* Airmont Classics, 1965.

Sizer, Theodore M. *Horace's Compromise: The Dilemma of the American High School.* Houghton Mifflin, 1992.

Smith, Betty. *A Tree Grows in Brooklyn.* HarperCollins, 1968.

Steinbeck, John. *Grapes of Wrath.* Viking/Penguin, 1976.

Steinbeck, John. *Of Mice and Men.* Bantam, 1983.

Stevenson, Robert Louis. *A Child's Garden of Verses.* Airmont Classics, 1969.

Strunk, William and E. B. White. *The Elements of Style.* Macmillan, 1979.

Taylor, Mildred D. *Roll of Thunder, Hear My Cry.* Bantam, 1984.

Thomas, Benjamin P. *Abraham Lincoln.* Random House, 1979.

Tolkien, J. R. R. *The Lord of the Rings* (3 volumes). Ballantine, 1986.

Tolstoy, Leo. *War and Peace.* Viking/Penguin, 1982.

Twain, Mark. *The Adventures of Huckleberry Finn.* Airmont Classics, 1962.

Warren, Robert Penn. *All the King's Men.* Harcourt Brace, 1983.

Watson, James D. *The Double Helix.* NAL/Dutton, 1969.

Weis, Margaret and Tracy Hickman. *Dragonlance Chronicles Series.* TSR, Inc., 1985.

White, Stewart Edward. *The Mountains.* (out of print)

Wiesel, Elie. *Night.* Bantam, 1982.

Wiggin, Kate Douglas. *Rebecca of Sunnybrook Farm.* Puffin Books, 1986.

Wilder, Laura Ingalls. *Little House on the Prairie.* HarperCollins, 1990.

A LIST OF BOOKS FOR YOUNG READERS

Compiled by the American Library Association

Books can stretch your mind and stimulate your imagination. In celebration of the Library of Congress' 1993-1994 national reading theme, "Books Change Lives," Book Links *magazine, a publication of the American Library Association, recommended these 30 titles for young readers. These books will help you think more about your world and introduce you to courageous people with inspiring stories. The books come in various paperback and hardcover editions and are available at public and school libraries and bookstores.*

Picture Books

Cooney, Barbara. *Miss Rumphius*. 1982. Viking, hardcover; Puffin, paper. 32 pages.

   Story and artwork meld in this tale of a girl who is charged by her grandfather to "make the world more beautiful." Recommended for Grades 2-4.

Fox, Mem. *Wilfrid Gordon McDonald Partridge*. Illustrated by Julie Vivas. 1985. Kane Miller, hardcover and paper. 32 pages.

   Readers will understand that gifts given from the heart are the most precious as they follow Wilfrid in his determination to help his friend Miss Nancy renew her memories. For Gr. 1-3.

Jukes, Mavis. *Like Jake & Me*. Illus. by Lloyd Bloom. 1984. Knopf, hardcover and paper. 32 pages.

   Much about contemporary family life and living is delicately incorporated into this amusing and understanding story about the changing relationship of a boy and his stepfather. For Gr. 2-4.

Shulevitz, Uri. *Dawn*. 1974. Farrar, hardcover and paper. 32 pages.

   A boy and his grandfather share the magic of a sunrise in expanding scenes that generate an awe of the natural world and a reverence for the miracle of life. For K-Gr. 3.

Williams, Vera. *A Chair for My Mother*. 1982. Greenwillow, hardcover; Mulberry, paper with audio cassette. 32 pages.

   After losing everything in a fire, a family saves its dimes to buy a warm and cozy armchair in a story that exudes familial affection and caring. For Gr. 1-3.

Folklore

Baker, Olaf. *Where the Buffaloes Begin*. Illus. by Stephen Gammell. 1989. Viking, hardcover and paper. 48 pages.

   The mythic tone of this story, enhanced by powerful black-and-white illustrations, communicates the native Americans' closeness to the natural elements of their world. For Gr. 2-5.

Hamilton, Virginia, ed. *The People Could Fly*: American Black Folktales. Illus. by Leo Dillon and Diane Dillon. 1985. Knopf, hardcover with audio cassette and paper. 192 pages.

   This comprehensive anthology of African-American folklore brings together a variety of tales especially selected for children, and includes illuminating historical notes. For Gr. 3-8.

Minard, Rosemary, ed. *Womenfolk and Fairy Tales*. 1975. Houghton, hardcover. 176 pages.

   Quick-witted, clever females, showing that they too can be heroes, star in this gathering of stories that includes old favorites, such as "Little Red Riding Hood," as well as the less familiar, such as "Kate Crackernuts."

Scieszka, Jon. *The True Story of the Three Little Pigs*. Illus. by Lane Smith. 1989. Viking, hardcover and boxed with cassette and stamp. 32 pages.

   Used in conjunction with a traditional version, such as James Marshall's Three Little Pigs (Dial), this inventive variation exemplifies how imagination can make a familiar story fresh and new. Gr. 1-4.

Yep, Laurence. *The Rainbow People*. Illus. by David Wiesner. 1989. HarperCollins, hardcover and paper. 208 pages.

   Twenty folktales of luck, cunning, heroism, and magic, gathered in the 1930s from Chinese immigrants, are retold with wit and vigor.

Fiction

Babbitt, Natalie. *Tuck Everlasting*. 1975. Farrar, hardcover and paper. 160 pages.

   In this quick-moving fantasy, the natural cycles of life and death are brought to the forefront as Winnie comes to understand the consequences of tasting water from a spring of life. For Gr. 5-7.

Lowry, Lois. *Number the Stars*. 1989. Houghton, hardcover; Dell, paper. 160 pages.

When 10-year-old Annemarie and her family help another family escape to Sweden, she becomes, in a small way, an agent of change—someone who makes a difference. Gr. 4-7.

Staples, Suzanne Fisher. *Shabanu: Daughter of the Wind*. 1989. Knopf, hardcover and paper. 256 pages.

Shabanu's life on the Cholistan desert in Pakistan is governed by her father and is far different from American readers' lives, but her hopes, dreams, and thoughts as she comes of age are much the same as theirs. Gr. 7-9.

Taylor, Mildred. *Roll of Thunder, Hear My Cry*. 1976. Dial, hardcover. 288 pages.

This compelling story inexorably pulls readers into the Logan family's life, forcing them to acknowledge the unfairness of the family's situation and moving them to admire the Logans' endurance. Gr. 6-9.

Yep, Laurence. *Dragonwings*. 1975. HarperCollins, hardcover and paper. 256 pages.

Yep's tale of a Chinese immigrant and his son's building a flying machine in early-twentieth-century San Francisco gives a fascinating portrayal of the time—and the great earthquake—from an immigrant's viewpoint. Gr. 5-7.

Biography

Burleigh, Robert. *Flight: The Journey of Charles Lindbergh*. Illus. by Mike Wimmer. 1991. Philomel, hardcover. 32 pages.

Lindbergh's 33-hour flight alone across the Atlantic stands as an example of courage and endurance in a world lacking strong role models and heroes.

Freedman, Russell. *Lincoln: A Photobiography*. 1987. Clarion, hardcover and paper. 160 pages.

With great fortitude, Lincoln struggled to get an education, build a law practice, become politically successful, and prevent this country from being torn in two. Gr. 3-8.

Latham, Jean L. *Carry On, Mr. Bowditch*. 1955. Houghton, hardcover and paper.

In this Newberry Medal winner, Latham presents Nat Bowditch, a self-educated man who triumphed over adversity and discovered a way to put mathematics to inventive use. Gr. 5-7.

Little, Jean. *Little by Little: A Writer's Education*. 1988. Viking, hardcover; Puffin, paper. 224 pages.

In this revealing autobiography a well-loved Canadian writer thoughtfully relates what it means to grow up "differntly abled." Gr. 5-8.

Parks, Rosa and James Haskins. *Rosa Parks: My Story*. Dial, hardcover. 191 pages.

By one day refusing to be shuttled to the back of the bus, Parks became not only a symbol for the African-American struggle for civil rights but also a role model for strength of purpose. Gr. 5-8.

Poetry

Adoff, Arnold. *All the Colors of the Race*. Illus. by John Steptoe. 1982. Lothrop, hardcover, 64 pages.

This lyrical tribute to children everywhere can be read as separate short pieces or as one continuous narrative. Gr. 1-4.

Carle, Eric. *Eric Carle's Animals, Animals*. Colleced by Laura Whipple. 1989. Philomel, hardcover. 96 pages.

Culturally diverse, visually exciting, invitingly accessible: this is all a poetry book should be. Preschool-Gr. 4.

Dunning, Stephen. *Reflections on a Gift of Watermelon Pickle and Other Modern Verse*. 1966. Lothrop, hardcover. 144 pages.

Stimulating and invigorating, this collection is an ideal vehicle for introducing older children to modern verse. Gr. 5-9.

Greenfield, Eloise. *Honey, I Love and Other Love Poems*. Illus. by Leo Dillon and Diane Dillon. 1978. HarperCollins, hardcover and paper. 48 pages.

This small volume containing poems of a young African-American girl's world and the people she knows is fast becoming a classic in the best sense of the word. Gr. 1-4.

Nye, Naomi Shihab. *This Same Sky: A Collection of Poems from around the World*. 1992. Four Winds, hardcover. 212 pages.

Nye's collection of verse by 129 poets from 68 different countries celebrates the natural world and its human and other animal inhabitants. Gr. 4-9.

Information

Durell, Ann and Marilyn Sachs, eds. *The Big Book for Peace*. Dutton, hardcover. 120 pages.

Stories, poems, and illustrations from various children's authors and artists demonstrate the wisdom of peace and the absurdity of fighting and focus on new ways to work and play together. Gr. 3-7.

Ehlert, Lois. *Planting a Rainbow*. 1988. Harcourt, hardcover. 32 pages.

The garden as a symbol for our planet Earth gives this graphically exciting, color-drenched book a significance beyond its simple planting theme. Preschool-Gr. 2.

Giblin, James. *From Hand to Mouth: Or, How We Invented Knives, Forks, Spoons & the Table Manners to Go with Them*. 1987. HarperCollins, hardcover. 96 pages.

Giblin stimulates thought as he adroitly links history, customs, and the development of civilization through his description of eating utensils. Gr. 3-6.

Laouber, Patricia. *Volcano: The Eruption and Healing of Mount St. Helens*. 1986. Bradbury, hardcover. 64 pages.

Text and photographs work well together to show how life returns after volcanic devastation, emphasizing the ongoing life cycles of nature. Gr. 3-7.

Myers, Walter Dean. *Now Is Your Time!: The African-American Struggle for Freedom*. 1991. HarperCollins, hardcover and paper. 320 pages.

The long, proud African-American struggle for freedom shines with a new light as seen through Myers' rich melding of story and biography. Gr. 5-9.

25 BOOKS THAT HAVE SHAPED READERS' LIVES: A LIST FROM THE CENTER FOR THE BOOK

The Adventures of Huckleberry Finn, by Mark Twain

Atlas Shrugged, by Ayn Rand

The Autobiography of Benjamin Franklin

The Autobiography of Malcolm X

The Bible

The Catcher in the Rye, J.D. Salinger

Charlotte's Web, by E.B. White

The Diary of a Young Girl, by Anne Frank

Don Quixote, by Miguel de Cervantes

Gone With the Wind, by Margaret Mitchell

Hiroshima, by John Hersey

How to Win Friends and Influence People, by Dale Carnegie

I Know Why the Caged Bird Sings, by Maya Angelou

Invisible Man, by Ralph Ellison

The Little Prince, by Antoine de Saint Exupery

Little Women, by Louisa May Alcott

The Lord of the Rings, by J.R.R. Tolkien

Roots, by Alex Haley

The Secret Garden, by Frances Hodgson Burnett

To Kill a Mockingbird, by Harper Lee

Treasure Island, by Robert Louis Stevenson

Walden, by Henry David Thoreau

War and Peace, by Leo Tolstoy

What Color is Your Parachute?, by Richard Nelson Bolles

The Wizard of Oz, by L. Frank Baum

READING PROMOTION PARTNERS OF THE LIBRARY OF CONGRESS

State Centers for the Book

By the end of the Books Change Lives campaign on December 31, 1994, the Center for the Book had affiliated centers in the following 29 states:

Alaska, Arizona, California, Colorado, Connecticut, Florida, Idaho, Illinois, Indiana, Iowa, Kansas, Kentucky, Louisiana, Michigan, Minnesota, Missouri, Montana, Nebraska, North Carolina, North Dakota, Ohio, Oklahoma, Oregon, Pennsylvania, Texas, Vermont, Virginia, Washington, and Wisconsin.

Organizations

By the end of the campaign, the following 135 organizations were Reading Promotion Partners of the Library of Congress:

AFL-CIO
Alpha Kappa Alpha Sorority, Incorporated
Altrusa International Foundation, Inc.
Alpha Phi Alpha Education Foundation
American Association for Adult and Continuing Education
American Association for the Advancement of Science
American Association of Community Colleges
American Association of Retired Persons
American Association of School Administrators
American Bar Association
American Booksellers Association
American Council on Education
American Federation of Teachers, AFL-CIO
American GI Forum of the United States
American Indian Library Association
American Library Association
American Mensa, Ltd.

American Postal Workers Union, AFL-CIO
Aspira Association, Inc.
Association for Supervision and Curriculum Development
Association of American Publishers
Association of American University Presses
Association of Booksellers for Children
Association of Junior Leagues International
Association of Research Libraries
Association of Youth Museums
Auxiliary of the National Rural Letter Carriers' Association
Baltimore City Literacy Corporation
Barbara Bush Foundation for Family Literacy
B'nai B'rith
Boy Scouts of America
Boys and Girls Clubs of America
Cartoonists Across Americas
Chautauqua Institution
Child Welfare League of America, Inc.
Children's Book Council
Children's Television Workshop
Christian Booksellers Association
Church and Synagogue Library Association
Cities In Schools, Inc.
Congress of National Black Churches
Corporation for Public Broadcasting
Correctional Education Association
Council for Early Childhood Professional Recognition
Delta Sigma Theta Sorority, Incorporated
Distance Education and Training Council
Federation of State Humanities Councils
First Book
4-H Youth Development Program - U.S. Department of Agriculture
Friends of Libraries U.S.A.
General Federation of Women's Clubs, International
Girl Scouts of the U.S.A.
Home & School Institute, Inc./Megaskills Education Center
International Association of Business Communicators
International Association of School Librarianship

International Book Bank, Inc.
International Reading Association
Jewish Book Council
KIDSNET
Kiwanis International
Laubach Literacy Action
Leo Clubs - Lions Clubs International
Library of America, The
Links, Inc., The
Literacy Volunteers of America
LULAC National Educational Service Centers, Inc.
Lutheran Church Library Association
Modern Language Association of America
Morning Start Institute
National Alliance of Black School Educators
National Alliance of Business
National Association for the Education of Young Children
National Association of Broadcasters
National Association of Colored Women's Clubs
National Association of Elementary School Principals
National Association of Partners in Education
National Association of Secondary School Principals
National Association of State Boards of Education
National Association of State Units on Aging
National Association of University Women
National Black Child Development Institute
National Book Foundation
National Catholic Educational Association
National Center for Family Literacy
National Clearinghouse for ESL Literacy Education
National Conference of Lieutenant Governors
National Council for the Social Studies
National Council of La Raza
National Council of Negro Women
National Council of State Directors of Adult Education
National Council of Teachers of English
National Council on the Aging
National Education Association
National Federation of Press Women
National Governors Association
National Indian Education Association

National Newspaper Foundation
National PTA
National School Boards Association
National School Public Relations Association
National Science Teachers Association
New Jersey Connection
Newspaper Association of America Foundation
OIC - Opportunities Industrialization Centers of America, Inc.
Parents Without Partners, Inc.
Phi Beta Kappa Society
Phi Beta Sigma Fraternity, Inc.
Phi Delta Kappa
Project Learning U.S. (PLUS)
Public Television Outreach Alliance
READAmerica
Reading Is Fundamental, Inc.
Ringling Bros and Barnum & Bailey Combined Shows, Inc.
SER - Jobs for Progress
Southern Newspaper Publishers Association
Special Libraries Association
Teachers & Writers Collaborative
Thomson Newspapers Corporation
U.S. Board on Books for Young People
U.S. Department of Defense Dependents' Schools
U.S. Department of Education
U.S. Department of Energy
U.S. Department of Health and Human Services
U.S. Department of Justice - Federal Bureau of Prisons
U.S. Department of Labor
U.S. Information Agency
U.S. National Commission on Libraries and Information Science (NCLIS)
U.S. Postal Service
United States Swimming
United Way of America
Washington Independent Writers
Weekly Reader Corporation
White House Conference on Libraries and Information Services Taskforce (WHCLIST))
Wider Opportunities for Women, Inc.
Women's National Book Association